Boatmen
of
Broadland

Margaret Dye

Dedication

This book is dedicated with affection to the Broadland boatmen
and boat yards who made Norfolk well known internationally in
the first half of the twentieth century and to the craftsmen of my
favourite modern boatyard, Nevill Towler's Anglo Marine
Services, who have built all my dinghies,
Wanderbug I, II, III and *IV*.

The Larks Press

Published by
the Larks Press, Ordnance Farmhouse, Guist Bottom,
Dereham, Norfolk NR20 5PF
01328 829207

Printed by the Lanceni Press
Garrood Drive, Fakenham, Norfolk

British Library Cataloguing-in-Publication Data
A catalogue record for this book is available from the
British Library

The author and publishers wish to thank all those who have
kindly allowed their photographs to be used for this book.

Other books by Margaret Dye:

Dinghy Cruising
Memories of Mill and Marsh
More Memories from the Marshes

CONTENTS

Thatched boat-sheds at Hickling

Foreword

When my husband and I sailed *Wanderer*, our much-travelled wooden Wayfarer dinghy, from her home waters of North Norfolk to the National Maritime Museum, Greenwich, in 1976, our emotions ranged from pride to sadness. A year previous to *Wanderer*'s last sail, I had been given the choice as to whether she should go to the museum or be given a Viking funeral. After much heart-searching, I felt that *Wanderer* would enjoy the companionship of other boats. They had much in common - good design and craftsmanship, and some good adventures to share.

However, I wept when we handed our dinghy over to the museum, so overwhelmed was I by our sense of loss. Basil Greenhythe, director of the museum, accepting *Wanderer*, whispered, 'A boat is the better part of one'. I was comforted. *Wanderer* continues to enrich our lives; we think of her often, and visit her regularly.

Historic boats, their design, construction and adventures are an integral part of our island story. As I sail around Broadland, I appreciate old and wooden boats. An especial thrill is to see a Hunter's Brown Boat passing by. This is the only fleet of yachts still together in their original setting at Hunter's Yard, Ludham; they are known internationally. Percy Hunter and sons Cyril and Stanley ran their fleet between 1932 and 68. The year following Percy's death, the yard was bought by Norfolk County Council, who sold on in 1996. The Norfolk Heritage Fleet Trust was then set up and now preserves these unique boats for all to enjoy.

The establishment of other boat yards, like that of Herbert Woods (the entrepreneur of Broads industry who set up his fleet around 1929 and had an enormous basin dug out at Potter Heigham, then just a small village with a parish staithe) and those of Collins, Applegates, Loynes, Brooms, Powles, Landamores, to

1

name just a few, gave impetus to the Boat Hire Industry. Its rapid development after the Second World War coincided with the fast growth in ownership of the private car, and so there was demand, and many beautiful launches and yachts were built.

By the 1970s, Norfolk was not only a place to holiday in; it was also a place to move to. Norfolk became the fastest-growing county in the U.K. Sadly, this population explosion brought an increase in pollution, traffic, pace of life and house-building. A better result was an increase in trade. Boat builders found work in restoring classic craft that had been sold out of the hire fleets into private hands, and many other craftsmen were kept busy servicing the needs of the incomers.

Protection of the Broads and maintenance of a healthy flora and fauna must be balanced with the increased demands for all kinds of recreation associated with Broadland. It is only when one is in danger of losing something special that one truly appreciates it, and so, as historic craft aged and disappeared from the much busier Broads, I felt a need to preserve the past. I wanted to know the special qualities that made Norfolk boatmen so enduring. How they lived, built boats, and earned a living at a time when Broadland was natural, unspoilt and unknown to the developers, became important to me.

The Broads are a unique collection of shallow man-made lakes and linking rivers. They happened as a result of peat digging between the twelfth and fifteenth centuries. One estimate was that over 900 million cubic feet of peat was excavated to make our twentieth century Broads. Fuel from peat was necessary in an area largely devoid of woodland. When, in the thirteenth and fourteenth centuries, the sea level rose, the area became flooded, and peat digging was abandoned. Alternative ways of making a living were developed as reedbeds and marshlands became established. The locals became adept at eel-trapping, fishing, wildfowling, and growing marsh crops, and they needed boats to travel about in.

The Broads were popularised as a holiday venue by Christopher Davies, who in his yacht *Swan* explored the area and wrote about his experiences, at a time when the Canal Age was giving way to the Age of the Railway.

Now, at the end of the century, sailing *Wanderbug* around Broadland is a perfect way to find out about and enjoy our nautical past. I also like to travel to other water-orientated areas. Wherever I go, it is the local boats that teach me most about other cultures and countries.

Very recently I visited Croatia, mainly to enjoy the restored city of Dubrovnik; however, I found the city harbour full of tourist boats; they dominated the few local fishing boats, so I looked elsewhere and found a means of exploring the lagoons and waterways of the River Delta region of Neretva.

Standing beside the stone walls of a deserted village house, I awaited transport. An ancient, black-tarred, open boat of clinker construction glided out from behind the reedbeds to tie up at a wooden quay. We were carried along reed-fringed waterways, where, every mile or so, we passed deserted villages, crumbling wharfs and rotting pontoons. The Neretva River Delta is a vast area of wetland, winding through the marshes. The reedbeds shelter and attract many species of bird life and animals. The local work boat, the *Trupice*, is no longer built, but two have been preserved to allow tourists to see the area. So similar are they to the Norfolk wherries that, as I looked out over the area, I could have thought I was back in Broadland, and it was only the distant vista of craggy mountains that reminded me I was actually on holiday.

Visiting ancient civilisations, such as Egypt, Greece, Turkey, Oman and Cyprus, I find it more rewarding to travel on local boats such as felucca, gullet and dhow. I get more insight into strange cultures and customs by watching local people working their local boats. It makes all the difference between being a tourist and a traveller.

This spring I revisited Egypt, mainly to enjoy the Cairo Museum, but I found I could not depart from this country, so very changed from my last visit some six years ago, without a walk beside the banks of the Nile. The sun sparkled on the blue waters and the strong winds ruffled its surface. One small felucca beat towards me, its dirty flax sails flapping as it changed direction. Suddenly the veil of time seemed to lift. I thought of the ancient Egyptians who used the river for trade and transport, from the primitive reed raft to the sumptuous dahabeeyah of the Eighteenth Dynasty. In fact the lines of the ships which sailed to Pwenet in Queen Hatshepsut's reign showed design features consistent with the basic river-boat model I had seen the previous day amongst Tutankhamen's

3

tomb artefacts in the museum.

The relationship between waterways and the craft that trade and travel on them and the people who designed and built these boats are like a never-ending history book through time and place. The preservation of this nautical past inspires feelings of pride and stability. In this modern global village, one can travel far, yet to come home to Norfolk and rush back to *Wanderbug* is one of the joys of my travelling life.

The author with *Wanderbug IV* at Hickling

Waldo Wellington Athelstan Beales

I first met Mr Beales in the early 1950s. Previously I hired half-deckers from Herbert Woods at Potter Heigham. Two pounds a day gave me the pleasure of enjoying *Never-can-tell* or *Wood White,* but as a beginner and self-taught sailor, I grew tired of tacking along the narrow bungalow-lined river. For a young teacher without a car, local bus transport from Norwich to the Broads was efficient, and I was told about some beautiful boats for hire from a yard at Hickling. So for a number of summers I rented out *Meadowsweet* or *Marigold* from Mr Beales. These two wooden half-deckers were clinker built, varnished with decking of non-slip lino. They were both 17 feet in length, with wooden mast and bamboo spars. Oars and a quant and baler were provided and bulky life-jackets. Buoyancy was in the form of oil-drums held beneath side decks with canvas straps. The sails were beautifully made, using creamy white Egyptian cotton.

Strong in my memory was the joy of stepping into a boat at 'Waldo's dyke' across the road from his bungalow and garage and sailing down the dyke and out on to Hickling Broad. A big blue stretch of water lay ahead beneath an endless blue sky. Big flocks of white swans would be feeding in the bays of the broad, and coots, ducks, butterflies and herons were all around. The fringing reedbeds were alive with birdsong. I learnt the delights of handling these half-deckers in all weathers, and never tired of the pleasure of feeling at one with such well-balanced boats. Occasionally, when I rang to book a dinghy, Mrs Beales, who did all the phone bookings, could only offer *Marguerite.* She was 18 feet in length and carvel built. I never enjoyed her as much. All three dinghies had their names painted on their transoms in gold, and outlined in grey. These well-used boats had been bought by Mr Beales from Woods of Potter Heigham after the war.

Over the seasons I got to know Waldo Beales as a friend. His manner was quite shy, with a gentle approach. Many a happy hour was spent in his immaculate boat shed, deep in conversation about boats. Coiled warps, beautiful blocks, and racks of tools lined the

Meadowsweet moored outside Hickling Sailing Club

walls of his green painted shed. Wanting to know more, I asked him to write down his experiences. Over the next few months he read to me his weekly writings. Pages of memories in beautiful copper plate writing were read out, but it was not about Broadland, but about his experiences during World War I. He called his story 'Battle of the Somme'. 'I feel easier now it's all down,' he said. I gave the pages to Mrs Beales when her husband died a short time later, at the age of 85 years. He never did write down his memories of growing up in Hickling, and he never told her of his writings.

I visited Mrs Beales several times the following season. She was a very active lady, maintaining the garden, and cycling around the village well into her 80th year. Billy Nudds, who helped Waldo Beales when his boat-hiring season grew, carried on with his visits too, and on many a sunny evening, as I returned from the Broad, by now sailing my own Wanderer dinghy, the couple would be sitting in the garden enjoying tea and home-made cake.

Billy Nudds was another village stalwart. He reclaimed the council dinghy park from a rubbish tip, beside the village staithe, and organized the berths and rental of the dinghy park, later organizing the building of two slipways. Often when I still rented Waldo's half-deckers, and was delayed returning because the wind dropped, leaving me to row back, I would come back into the dyke in the dark. A hand would shoot out of the darkness and catch the boat. 'Had a good day, Marg?' was all he said. After Waldo's death, Billy carried on helping with the boats, and cutting the lawn and hedges of Mrs Beales bungalow, as well as the village graveyard and bowling green. Billy died in 1993, at the age of 85 years, and he was active until the day of his death. Billy's hearse left the village church after the funeral service, and on its way to the graveyard went by the dinghy park, and paused. Billy would have liked that. He was proud of being associated with that special place. Mrs Beales now lives in a nursing home, and enjoys her retirement there.

Waldo Beales' interest in boats must have been inherited from his father and grandfather. He was born in 1897, in the Pleasure Boat Inn. George and Annie had eleven children, and Waldo was the last but one. There were seven boys and four girls. They all attended the local village school in Hickling village. George, Waldo's father, kept the Pleasure Boat from 1880-1911 and hired out a variety of rowing and small sailing boats, whilst his mother took in guests. As the family grew, the parents slept on the floor. Four of Waldo's brothers emigrated to America at the end of the First World War, looking for a better life.

George and Annie Beales outside the Pleasure Boat Inn, Hickling, with six of their children - Waldo is sitting with the dog.

Waldo's grandfather, also George, was a real worker. He owned the wherry *Emily*, built around the late 1880s, and made many long and seaman-like journeys from Hickling staithe to Yarmouth and back, carrying coal, wheat, hay, straw, beans and litter. *Emily* was named after a sister in the Beales family, and George, Waldo's father, as a lad of thirteen years, sometimes skippered his father's wherry, and was crewed by his brother Edward, aged nine years. On one occasion in 1873, George, brother Edward, and a young friend sailed from Hickling to Yarmouth to witness a visit by the Prince of Wales. The adventure is told in *Life and Sport on the Norfolk Broads,* by Oliver Ready, written in the early 1900s.

Date of voyage	Nav. Up Down	Vessel	Master	Qty	Description of Freight	Amount Toll			Date	How paid	Cash Book No.	Amount Recd.		
						£	s	d				£	s	d
1887														
July 21	UP	EMILY	G. Beales	15 Tons	Coal	-	1	3						
July 27	UP	EMILY	G. Beales	16 Tons	Coal	-	1	4						
Aug 4	UP	EMILY	G. Beales	16 Tons	Coal & Pollard	-	1	7	Sept 7 1887	By Cash	1	-	4	2
Sept 7	UP	EMILY	G. Beales	15 Ton 30 Combs 1 Barrel	Coal Maize Parafin	-	2	0						
Sept 14	UP	EMILY	G. Beales	15 Ton 2 Barrels	Coal & Parafin	-	1	9						
Sept 22	UP	EMILY	G. Beales	15 Ton 1/2 Ton 2 Bits	Coal Pollard Soda	-	1	5						
Sept 30	UP	EMILY	G. Beales	15 Tons	Coal	-	1	3	Oct 4 1887	By Cash	3	-	6	5
Oct 5	DOWN	EMILY	G. Beales	56 Combs 20 Combs	Beans Wheat	-	1	3						
Oct 8	UP	EMILY	G. Beales	10 Ton 1 Ton 10 Combs 6 Barrels	Coal sharps Maize Parafin	-	2	8						
Oct 14	UP	EMILY	G. Beales	10 Ton 2 Ton 1 Ton	Coal Cake Pollard	-	1	4						
Oct 27	DOWN	EMILY	G. Beales	50 Combs	Wheat	-	-	10	Nov 2 1887	By Cash	5	-	6	1
Nov 5	UP	EMILY	G. Beales	12 Ton 4 Ton	Coal & Pollard	-	1	8						
Nov 10	DOWN	EMILY	G. Beales	70 Combs 1 Ton	Wheat & Barley Hay & Straw	-	1	5						
Nov 11	UP	EMILY	G. Beales	15 Tons	Coal	-	1	3						
Nov 18	DOWN	EMILY	G. Beales	40 Combs 3/4 Ton	Beans & Litter	-	-	10	Dec14 1887	By Cash	6	-	5	2

Extract from the River Bure Tolls Ledger for 1887 showing journeys made by Waldo's grandfather George in *Emily*

In 1916 *Emily* was involved in a collision at Six Mile Bottom, on the River Bure, between Runham and Yarmouth. The wherry sank, carrying a load of 25 tons of corn; there was a high wind blowing, when the collision with another wherry happened, and at the subsequent court case, much nautical swearing was heard between the two wherrymen. Horbough of Norwich raised the wherry, stripped her down, and used her as a lighter.

In those days, the winters could be very severe, and ice on the Broad could be many inches thick. Wherryman George Beales was a very fine skater; he was also a very religious man, who would never sail on a Sunday. Wherever he happened to berth his wherry on a Saturday night, he would walk across the marshes to the nearest village chapel to worship on the Sabbath.

Waldo's first two boats were bought in the late 1920s. Both were 14 feet long, clinker built, and pointed at both ends, varnished, with rubber matting over the floorboards, and with three seats. They were provided with heavy mud-weights, and, being used for fishing, were often out all night. They had no names, merely being called No.1 and No.2. After the war, small Seagull outboards were provided. Three rowing boats were bought around 1937. Each was

9

**The Pleasure Boat in 1890 before it was extended.
A wherry is moored in the dyke.**

about 14 foot long, clinker built, varnished, with three seats, the rear one having a back-rest. These were built by Loynes, and Waldo towed them back from Wroxham to Hickling, sleeping overnight in them, beneath a sail cover. Two were named after his wife and daughter, *Iris* and *Pat*, whilst the third was called *Joan*. Each name was hand-painted in gold by his nephew Stanley, who worked for his uncle; later David Platten continued this practice. These fishing and rowing boats were kept until about 1974.

About 1950, Waldo bought three dinghies; they were built by Moores, hard chine, 11 foot 6 inches long, varnished mahogany, with a centre plate, wood mast, and brown lug sails. These were designed for the sailing beginner, and were simple to rig and control. Their names were *Reed Warbler*, *Marsh Warbler* and *Willow Warbler*. There was good stowage and wet mooring for this fleet of boats, because Waldo had built large boat-houses around 1927. (He built his bungalow in 1929.)

During the Second World War, Waldo knew great hardship, as fishing and sailing were not allowed on the Broad; indeed,

Hickling Broad was staked with posts and wire to prevent the landing of enemy seaplanes. Private cars could not be used, and so the boat hire and garage were hard to keep going. However, after the war, the business flourished again, and Waldo could not get enough boats to satisfy the demand. People were optimistic, had time and money, and wanted to enjoy both, so Waldo's rowing, fishing boats, dinghies and half-deckers were very popular.

The fact that Waldo ran a small garage alongside his boat hiring happened mainly by chance. Joining the First World War effort, by lying about his age, and enlisting when only seventeen, he saw active service in the last year of the war. He was invalided out and spent six months in hospital before returning to Hickling, taking a machinery course in Norwich after recuperation. This resulted in the setting up of petrol pumps and a workshop, built on swampy waste ground, close to the village staithe. So both businesses grew up together and the customers were well looked after. The simple bungalow that Waldo built about 1929 was on rough ground used to store carts. Stones and cobbles infilled the bungalow's base.

Pat, Waldo's only child, grew up playing on the village staithe, later rowing and sailing any kind of boat that her father gave her. As she grew up, she became a much- sought-after racing crew for local sailors; especially she remembers enjoying sailing with Mick Richardson in his well-known *Slipstream* boat, and also crewing and winning races with John Perryman.

'Don't glorify my father,' said Pat, many years on. 'My father loved to see his customers happy.' Now, a qualified teacher of art and close to retirement, she is enjoying her previously thwarted career as an interior designer. Her parents' house and workshop is being modernized and re-designed in keeping with the Broadland area. Pat's husband has repaired and restored Waldo's green shed, and all his tools are cared for within it.

The local sailing club, with a marvellous thatched club-house overlooking the Broad, originated at the instigation of Waldo and Jimmy Turner, another boat builder in the village. Together they wanted to organize racing on a Sunday morning for local men. After a meeting at the Pleasure Boat Inn, the informal racing group became an organized club, and each Sunday morning during the season, a racing programme was established for class A and B. Waldo often took part in one of his half-deckers.

Now, at the end of the 1990s, the work of Waldo is remembered. The Hickling Sailing Club is flourishing, and the Broad is once again enjoying clear water and returning bird life, feeding on the abundant weed, recalling the days of the 1930s, when Waldo and his young wife would sail across to Catfield dyke where the water was especially clear, to swim and eat breakfast.

The village is now enjoying many weekend and daily visitors, and large numbers of incomers are restoring village cottages with care and cash for their second or retirement homes. Not so long ago, in the early 1940s, life was not too easy. Ben Lacey, a retired seaman, lived in old upturned hull of a black tarred boat in a very neglected area at the point of the village staithe. He wore a tattered old fisherman's guernsey, had a flat cap, and sported a grey stubble beard. His dog was a black and white mongrel, called Poype. When his home was burnt down, Ben was moved to a floating, grey houseboat, on the left-hand side of the back dyke. Previously Miss Turner, the famous ornithologist, had owned the boat. When Ben became very old and ill, Mrs Beales would send her small daughter to the houseboat to take him hot soup. Many years on, Pat still recalls the bad smells surrounding the old man and the filth surrounding his home.

Boats for hire, a peaceful day on the Pleasure Boat dyke.

Billy Andrews

Pat Simpson first introduced me to Billy Andrews. His family came to Norfolk from Nottingham in 1945. There was no history of sailing in the family, yet, living as far from the sea as is possible in England, his father, Miles, owned an off-shore boat, taking her regularly down the Trent and across to Holland. When the Second World War broke out, Miles sailed his boat back to England and left it at Blakeney, with Stratton Long, saying as he departed, 'See you after the war'. He then served his country in the Navy in the R.N.V.R.

After the war, seeking for a new start in life, Miles came to Norfolk looking for a boat yard. At that time most villages had their own staithes, and close to one of these at Stalham was one of the oldest boat yards. A site here was owned by Captain Kettlewell, and Miles bought it from him.

Originally the yard had been started by Joe Teasel around 1835. He built wherries, specializing in smaller ones that could be used on the Dilham and North Walsham Canal, nothing bigger than twenty tons. By reputation, these smaller wherries were not successful, but when the Southgate family took over the boat yard, they continued the building of many wherries and achieved a high reputation for their work.

So Miles Simpson carried on working in the boat yard, always living in Staithe House. 'It was a lovely place for a boy to grow up,' said Pat, his son. The yard was then known as Stalham Yacht Services, and the tradition of building and hiring yachts and motor cruisers continued.

In 1975 Pat and his wife, Jenny, took over the boat yard. They met whilst working on charter yachts in the Caribbean; both are qualified yacht masters. Their two sons are at university and the younger one hopes to take up a career in yachting, possibly in ocean racing.

Whilst all the wooden boats in the hire fleet have been replaced by G.R.P. ones, there are many beautiful and historic wooden yachts in the yard, owned by private individuals, and these

13

are maintained and stored by the boat yard services. Particularly eye-catching sits a ship's boat in a wet mooring. Pat found it at Snape and brought it back to his yard, where a film crew used it to make the films based on Arthur Ransome's *Swallows and Amazons* and *The Big Six.*

Some of the remnants of buildings used in the wherry-trading times of the staithe can still be seen in the yard. Sheds to store corn, coal, lime and other agricultural products are no longer by the riverside, but the beer store and the brick shed that once stored timber live on in people's memories. Pat has built a new shed on the site of the old wherry shed.

Pat walked me through his immaculate yard to a small, brick prefabricated bungalow, and introduced me to Mr Billy Andrews. I have rarely spent such a happy morning. The years were swept aside while Billy, an octogenarian with a sharp wit, clarity of memory and an optimistic nature, totally charmed me.

Billy was born in 1912, in Ford's Cottage, Stalham. His first trip in a wherry was when he was eight years old. His grandfather had been a wherryman, and his father, by trade a shoemaker whose work shrank when cheap imported Italian footwear flooded into U.K., went to the granary and turned to the wherries to make a living. He was paid 1d per ton to take goods along the Dilham canal. 'Possibly our family contains more than three generations of wherrymen,' said Billy, but we could not find any records.

Billy started work in 1926; his first pay packet was 4/6d for a forty-seven-hour week. He was employed as a boat-builder at Southgate and Sons' yard. Mr R. Southgate and sons Edward and George operated at Sutton Staithe yard, also using premises at Stalham. In their heyday, three to four wherries were produced annually. Billy worked for the Southgates until both yards were taken over in 1938; then he continued with the new owners. Billy was taught his trade by his governors, and he learnt his skills whilst repairing wherries and helping to build yachts. 'In 1926 I felt very lucky to be learning the boat-building trade', said Billy. 'Most people worked on farms'. He was trained how to clean and sharpen his woodworking tools. 'Your tools are not sharp enough,' he was sometimes told. His boss would sharpen a chisel, then run it down his forearm until the hairs on it curled over. 'That's properly sharp boy,' he was told. There were no power tools, nor electric light,

A wherry moored at Stalham Staithe.

Photograph kindly lent by the Museum of the Broads

15

just oil lamps. 'We used to take a piece of wood, put three nails in it, wedge the candle between them and walk about working by the light of the candle.' Candles were bought by the hundredweight. An early job Billy remembers enjoying was to sit overlooking the river, rolling okum strips on his knee. 'Three different sizes were made for use in caulking different parts of yachts,' Billy explained.

A boat-building shed in the middle of the boat yard, now gone, was where the men built some wherries, although others were built on the riverside banks. 'We had to build the boats in two parts,' explained Billy. 'The shed wasn't high enough so we built the hull first, then the keel separately, and put them together outside, near the slipway. The hull had to be lifted, the keel centralized, then the two were bolted together. Sometimes the keels got damaged in the shallow Stalham channel, and had to be taken off.'

Billy told me the procedure for 'firing a wherry'. The old boat would be laid on edge on the banks of the staithe. One man would run a rush brush over the hull to dry off the wood. The second man went along the hull covering its surface with boiling pitch, carried in a bucket. The third man fired it up, whilst the fourth went behind him waving a damp cloth over the timbers to subdue the flames. By this method the old scum was taken off the timbers; they would be cleaned, sealed, waterproofed and hardened, and the wherry would be ready to work again.

One of the first yachts that Billy worked on was the *Dorothy*. Masts, spars and blocks were all made by hand. *Dorothy* was completed in 1927. Whenever money was available, the yard

Yacht DOROTHY

This sloop-rigged, carvel-built, graceful white Yacht is similar in appearance to the "Diana" shown on the previous page. Her interior arrangement, however, is slightly different, as the plan reproduced below indicates.

The "Dorothy" has a length of 30 ft., a beam of 8 ft. 6 in., and a draught of 2 ft. 10 in. She will float in practically any navigable water in Broadland.

Her two cabins, that aft measuring 6 ft. 3 in. and the fore-cabin 6 ft., are separated by the wash-basin and self-emptying w.c. Each cabin is fitted with spring berths and drawers beneath, and the fore-cabin is furnished with a dressing-table and cupboard. The cabin top

lifts, giving 6 ft. head-room when up, and 5 ft. when down. The cabins are well supplied with shelves. There is also a cot-mattress in the forepeak. The cooking locker, containing oil-stove and primus, is in the well, which is fitted with a waterproof awning, which at night or in inclement weather converts the well almost into another cabin.

This yacht sleeps seven persons comfortably, and is well ventilated. All necessary utensils for cruising and sleeping, except towels, are supplied.

There is a Centre-board Sailing Dinghy.

Terms per week, unattended—

Periods (see p. 12)—
A £7.   B £8 10s.   C £10

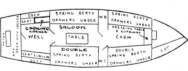

Entry for *Dorothy* in Southgates' catalogue, late 1930s.

16

started a new yacht. Private work and repairs were often taken on to raise extra cash and then more work would continue on the yacht. The *Diana* was an even bigger yacht, and the last big one to be built at the Southgate yard; the year was 1929. *Diana*'s length was 30 feet, her beam was 8 feet 6 inches; having a shallow draught of 2 feet 10 inches, she was designed for the shallow local waters. The yacht could sleep seven people, and for between £7 10s and £10 10s a week, depending on the season, she could be hired out with a centre-board sailing dinghy, unattended. 'We were behind with the building schedule, and as we quanted her down the river from Sutton to her sailing base at Stalham, I was fitting moulds and completing details, so that the yacht could be in time for the Saturday hire. There was no time for sailing trials,' Billy beamed broadly, as if the memory still gave him pleasure. 'I loved boats,' he said. 'I knew nothing else. I would have worked for nothing.'

Between 1934 and 1936 Billy Andrews ran the yard for Southgates and when it was sold he continued to run it for Captain

***Diana*, the last big yacht to be built at the Southgate Boat Yard, Sutton, in 1929**

17

Kettlewell, from 1937-8. In 1939 war came and the government closed the yard. The men were given instructions to bore holes in the yachts to ensure that the enemy could not use them.

Billy was sent to Cambridge for a medical to decide where he would be sent for the war years. 'What are you doing here?' said an official who pulled Billy out of the queue. Billy recognised the official as an ex-Broads boat-hirer whose family he had taught to sail on Barton Broad for three weeks each summer regularly for many years, 'when summers were summers,' smiled Billy.

'I m going to join the Navy,' replied Billy.

'No, you are not, you have varicose veins. I have a different job for you.' So Billy was taken out of the line of men. 'I went to the top of the tree, and was sent to train at Wiltshire,' chuckled Billy. 'I completed my war work as a wireless operator working on dispatches'.

In 1945, when the war ended, Billy received a message out of the blue, 'Come back to the yard, nobody can rig the yachts.' 'So I was never out of work,' said Billy. 'The yard was in a terrible mess; we had to sort out quants, oars, blocks, sails, and clean up the sails before the yachts could be rigged.' As foreman of the yard, Billy helped Captain Kettlewell re-establish the boat yard. When Miles Simpson bought it, Billy retained his position. He remembers the time when Pat, Miles' young son, was left in his pram, in the sheds, for Billy to keep an eye on. 'I changed his nappies more than once,' Billy chuckled.

After the war, Mr and Mrs Andrews could not afford a house in Stalham, so they moved to Smallburgh, where they lived in a cottage for twenty-five years. When Mr Simpson suggested they moved back to Stalham, they bought a prefab house for one hundred pounds. This was moved to the village and erected overlooking the Simpsons' boat yard.

'I knew everybody and I loved the boats,' said Billy. The cosy, beautifully-cared-for, brick prefab is home for the eighty-seven-year-old ex-boat-builder. His wife died three years ago, on their sixty-fifth wedding anniversary, and the home is full of happy memories of a long, busy life; photographs of the family and the tankard presented to Billy to commemorate fifty years with Hoseasons are prominent. Billy retired in 1978.

Billy Andrews' mind is very active and he loves to share his memories. 'The river was so clean and clear in those days, we used to drink it and wash in it,' he recalled. 'The visitors were lovely people. The men would be dressed in white flannels, and the ladies wore white dresses. They would hire a boat and take it up to Barton Broad. The families would enjoy a picnic. They would be content to sit in a boat all day, maybe reading or painting. There was such harmony. They watched the coots and the fish, and listened to the birds in the reedbeds and watched the butterflies and dragonflies darting over the great beds of water-lilies. They were so contented. The families would come by train straight to the yard, often from the Midlands. There were no telephones, so bookings were done by letter or telegram. Often families rented cottages as well as a boat. There were four cottages near the granary. You could see the village people sitting in the gardens with the visitors. Sometimes they would share a meal together. When families hired a wherry, there would be a skipper and steward in attendance. A piano on board would have been played in the evenings, and the sound would drift across the water.' During the busy fourteen to sixteen week summer season, a lot of Billy's time would be taken up with the hirers. 'I would take them up the quiet reaches of the River Ant, or up to Barton, or maybe they wanted to visit the local regattas, or maybe have sailing instruction. Sometimes if we had a long day afloat, the scud would come down over Barton, then I would drift back across the broad; when I heard the chimes on the clock on Barton Hall, I knew the way home. There was always so much harmony and tranquillity in our days afloat.'

Billy's memories took him even further back. 'We had three saws each,' he explained. 'We had one saw to give a wide, straight cut, the second saw cut round the bends in the wood, whilst the third was long and narrow and used to cut the stem out. It took two men days to cut out the keels. The garboard plank would be cut by hand, one man either side of the plank. We didn't waste a thing. The building sheds all had their corners where items were placed. In one corner was wood waiting to have copper nails extracted, in another would be wood saved for special purposes.'

'We're going out today,' said Billy's governor. By now the tide of Billy's memory was receding even further. I was told how the fledgling boat-builder and his boss would cycle around the farms, looking for trees to buy. 'You could build a fine yacht out of that...

There's a nice keel in there....Look at those lovely knees in there.'

So the tree would have a dab of paint to identify it; later it might be bought from the farmer, and the wood taken to the yard. 'Timbers would be laid down for five years before being used,' explained Billy. 'As the wood dried, the colours would come out. Larch, pine and silver birch would look beautiful after a year or so. Some families would visit us, wanting a dinghy built, and would walk round the timber shed and select their wood; it was always the ladies that chose.'

A twelve-foot clinker built rowing dinghy could be built for one pound a foot and a sailing dinghy for twenty-five shillings a foot. The yachts in the hire fleet were rented out for about two pounds per bunk per week, and the rowing boats for two shillings a day.

Dove and Wren yachts at Stalham Staithe

Museum of the Broads

The yachts in the hire fleet usually were given girls' names. 'We were so proud of our boats,' enthused Billy. 'The hire fleet got a primer and three coats of varnish, while the private ones got nine coats. They were cut down and down, and in the end, they looked perfect.' Every can of varnish was dated. Varnish was bought in tubs and transferred to cans, which were bedded in sawdust then matured for two years before being used. 'You could get drunk on it when it was really mature,' said Billy grinning wickedly. 'You had to peel it off your lips, it coated candle-light, and we were proud of our work.'

Some boats possibly had bits of wood from the old wherries. Billy explained that wherries from the yard would pick up broken-down boats at Darby's Hard, Yarmouth, and the wood was brought back to the staithe to sell off at four shillings a load. Some of the old timbers were used in making boat sheds. Copper nails were also extracted and re-used. Nothing was wasted.

Billy's attention turned to customers in the past. 'We built *Swallow*, a racing punt, at Sutton, for Mr Batchelor, the artist, and we built lighters for the Boardman family of How Hill. One job I did every year was private work. I cycled from Stalham to collect a half-decker kept at Waxham Bridge farm. Every year, when the family's holiday was over, I would sail the boat back to Stalham for winter storage. Sometimes I got as far as Potter Heigham or to Ludham Bridge before mooring up and cycling home for the night. The following season, I would repeat the trip in reverse and make sure the boat was ready for the family to enjoy when they returned for their holiday.'

Stalham Broad in 1926, looking towards Southgates' Boat Yard
Photograph kindly lent by the Museum of the Broads

I asked Billy who taught him to sail. 'Nobody,' he replied. 'I expect I fell into the water at the beginning, climbed back into the boat and carried on.'

Meeting Billy Andrews revived my interest in trading wherries and talking, months later, to Sid Wren, another well-known boat-builder of the Herbert Woods era, I learnt that the wherrymen could judge the weather pretty accurately and when crossing Breydon bringing a cargo up to Norwich they would hudge when they could drop off their wherry keels on the mud and proceed up to Norwich. Sailors coming up behind would know who had got ahead by the line of keels left lying in the shallows. Alternatively wherry keels could be unbolted from the hulls and towed behind.

During another mardle John Perryman told me that there were three bolts securing the keel to the wherry hull. 'Water poured into the hold unless the bungs replacing the bolts were replaced smartly,' he said. 'It might take twenty minutes to get rid of the keel, but a hell of a lot longer to put it back on again.'

How fortunate I am to have met Billy Andrews. He has deepened my appreciation of Broadland. My sailing days ahead will be given new meaning.

Yachts LASSIE 1, 2, 3

"LASSIE 1"

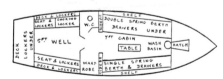

These yachts are smart Una-rigged boats. Having only a mainsail, which may be hoisted or lowered from the well, these boats are admirably suited for novices possessing little knowledge of sailing. Their length is 20 ft., and beam 8 ft., making them a convenient size to handle safely.

The single cabin is snugly fitted with a double and a single berth, making sleeping accommodation for three persons. The cabin also contains a shut-off patent flushing w.c. on the port side, and a wardrobe opposite. There is plenty of storage space under the berths and in the lockers under the seats in the well.

The cooking locker is in the well.

All requisites for sleeping and cruising for three persons are supplied.

A feature of the "Lassie" class is that an outboard motor can be fixed if desired at £2 10s. per week extra.

Terms per week, unattended—
Periods (see p. 12)—A. £3 15s   B £4 15s.   C £6.

Lassie I, built complete for £100 in 1931

Maurice Davey

Maurice Davey was born in Oby Mill in 1914. The family had lived and attended to the mill for the past one hundred years. Its first engine ran on steam, then in due course a diesel engine followed.

Maurice's father was a marshman, a carpenter and a smallholder, keeping cows and chickens and running a dairy. Some of his produce he sold to people travelling the river. Wiseman's farm was also under his supervision.

There were three children, two boys and a girl. Maurice and his brother Herbert learnt to row on the river when very young. In a very old boat they would row to the end of the dyke and then walk to the village school at Upton. When their boat was smashed in 1926, they built themselves another one. While they were building their replacement Herbert Woods lent the boys a sailing dinghy, so they taught themselves to sail.

Herbert built a model yacht which so impressed the professionals that he was taken on by Herbert Woods. Two years later Maurice followed on to serve his apprenticeship. He was just fourteen years old. One of his fellow apprentices was Jimmy Turner.

Herbert Davey with his model yacht, 1927

23

As young boys working at Woods' yard by the river, they learnt by looking; they watched the wherry traders and the pleasure wherries sail by and they absorbed their design features and sailing qualities. Once Maurice was by the river bank at Oby Mill on a Sunday morning and remembers hearing the church bells ringing from five church towers: Upton, Ranworth, Horning, Martham and Thurne.

In 1929 he was involved in cruiser-building on the west side of Potter Heigham bridge, on the east bank. The apprentices worked under the watchful eye of the foreman, Ben Balls. Sometimes the work was done in the open and sometimes simple sheds were used. Also in this year some marshes were bought at Potter Heigham and dug out by hand by about a dozen unemployed marshmen who earned 28s. a week for their labours. The result was the beginnings of 'Broads Haven'. The digging of this basin was completed in 1930 and Maurice and his brother helped dig out smaller basins and watched the water pour into them as the entrance to the river was excavated by the Horbough's dredger. (This was not achieved without mishap, for the dredger's driver damaged his hand badly when the chain broke.)

Workshops, storage sheds, office block and water tanks went up in quick succession and so, from 1935 onwards, the men and their boys had some degree of comfort. Already the yard had a fine reputation for building the 'Lady' class boats and also the 'Light' motor cruisers. In the 1930s forty per cent of all the Broads yachts were for hire with skippers and attendants as part of the deal, so the hiring trade was a good provider of employment for local men.

Yachts for hire at Martham Boat Yard

24

In his first job at the yard Maurice was involved with 'Norfolk' dinghies. They were gunter rig, with bamboo masts and spars. Hulls were of clinker construction. This dinghy was designed by Herbert Woods in response to the demand for a cheaper boat than the fourteen foot 'International' class then costing around £400 or so. 'Norfolk' dinghies were costed out at about £65. Two or three were built annually from 1931 onwards and a fleet of around 80 'Norfolks' was established eventually. The last one, No.86, was completed in 1968. 'It took two weeks to build a Norfolk,' recalled Maurice, 'I worked on one side and Jimmy Turner worked on the other; Walter Wood varnished them as they were completed'. Maurice's wage at that time was 8s. weekly, - 'Four bob for me and four for my mother.'

Maurice's mother grew tired of the hardships of living in the mill. It was a constant battle to keep the family dry and fed in such basic conditions. There was nowhere to dry wet clothes, and bread had to be baked three times a week in a wall oven. The two boys slept in a room in the rafters, reached by a ladder which was withdrawn once they were in bed. 'So once we were up there, we had to stay,' said Maurice. At last the family renovated a bungalow and moved away from the mill.

Maurice left Woods once his apprenticeship was completed. 'They couldn't pay a man's wage,' so he went to Eastex of Acle in 1937 and helped to build *Royal Oak,* a famous cruiser.

Maurice married in 1939 and he and his wife lived in a tied cottage in Potter Heigham where their son was born. When their landlord wanted his cottage he told the young couple that there were plenty of huts on the airfield at Ludham where they could live. Fortunately a new home was offered by Stalham Council and life became easier for them.

After the outbreak of war in 1939, Maurice returned to Woods' yard to help with building naval boats whilst awaiting his posting in the Navy. In 1943 he was drafted to Lerwick. Lying in bed in a Nissen hut feeling the walls move in the 100 miles per hour winds that raged outside was a new experience for the raw recruits. Despite having a wife and young son in Norfolk, Maurice enjoyed his time in the Shetlands and made friends with the locals. His work involved general repair to all the boats used in the war effort. 'That could mean anything from a submarine to a motor torpedo boat, and the Norwegians sent their craft to Lerwick for repairs too'. Once he was called upon to take the responsibility of doing a complete survey of a vessel. 'One hundred men's lives were at stake as a result of that survey,' he said.

Maurice served his country in the Shetlands for over two years before returning to Norfolk where he was demobbed in 1946.

Way back in the days when he had been working at Woods' yard, Maurice and some of his friends had talked and dreamed endlessly about having their own business. So in 1946 the dream became a reality. 'Martham Boat Building and Development Co. Ltd.' was set up comprising James Brown, Frank Skoyles, Derwent Wright and Maurice Davey. They moved to a yard at Martham owned by J. C. Pritchard whilst Jimmy Brown owned a site with sheds close by in Martham village. Jimmy was the managing director - 'He was the brains of the enterprise,' said Maurice - whilst Wright, Skoyles and Davey were directors. So began a remarkable increase in the 'June' launch fleet. 'Jimmy was a great asset; he raked in the contracts, and we all worked all hours.'

A 20 foot fishing boat made for Mr J. Dyble.
He caught almost enough herring on his first trip
to pay for the boat.

26

Japonica **under full sail**

Maurice was the main boat-designer. 'I seemed to know what was required; manoeuvrability and the ability to pass through Potter Heigham bridge were my main concerns. My first designs were scout boats of 12 to 16 feet. Then came 30 foot sailing cruisers, next the 'Janet' class, followed by 'Janes', 'Janices', 'Judiths' and 'Juliettes'. We also had five houseboats and bought in some Woods half-deckers.'

Maurice gave full credit to the directors' wives, the ladies who cleaned the boats and the men who built and repaired them, also to the men who guided the customers through Potter bridge to give them a good start to their holidays.

In 1947 a large hangar was purchased from Swanton Morley Airfield and all four directors worked all night to erect it. From then on work could be done in greater comfort. Maurice's whole family was involved in building up the operation. His wife washed and aired three hundred sheets a week. Cyril, her son, collected the linen off the boats and helped his mother wash and iron them. They were all completed by Sunday night and returned to the boats.

The 1950s were years of rapid growth for all at the boat yard and the fleet grew to over one hundred, but one of Jimmy Brown's

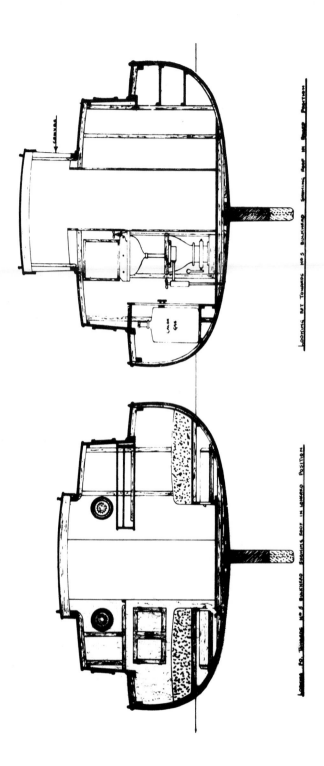

LOOKING AFT TOWARDS N° 5 BULKHEAD SHEWING ROOF IN RAISED POSITION

TRANSVERSE SECTION FOR SAILING CRUISER *JAPONICA*
Designed by M.DAVEY. Drawn by A. CARMICHAEL, A.I.N.A.
Built by MARTHAM BOAT, BUILDING & DEVELOPMENT C° LTD.
SCALE :- 1IN = 1FT.

LOOKING FD TOWARDS N° 4 BULKHEAD SHEWING ROOF IN RAISED POSITION

Maurice Davey's designs for the *Japonica*

dreams was to own a wherry. And so *Hathor* was bought. *Hathor* had been built in 1905 by Daniel Hall of Reedham for Helen and Ethel Colman, daughters of J. Colman, the founder of the Colman's mustard firm. Their younger brother, Alan, was a frail boy and in 1896 he travelled to Egypt to convalesce. It was hoped that the dry Egyptian air and heat would improve his 'delicacy of the lungs'. It proved a vain hope for he died in Luxor the following year, having enjoyed a trip down the Nile on an Egyptian sailing boat *Hathor* (meaning 'goddess of love and joy'). Seven years later, the Colman sisters decided to name their new wherry *Hathor* in memory of their brother. The interior design was based on Egyptian mythology and hieroglyphics; lotus flower motifs were inlaid into sycamore to beautify the cabin, whilst Egyptian animals and symbols decorated the doors.

Hathor was launched in 1905. Later Claud Hamilton bought her, then, some years on, the wherry was bought for Martham Development Co. They used her as a houseboat as well as for sailing trips.

'That was the only time I skived off work,' said Cyril, Maurice's younger son. 'We took the *Hathor* to Coltishall for a week before the season began. Each day different men from the yard were taken for a day's sail.'

'The Coltishall Anchor kept open all that week,' said his father, his eyes twinkling at the memory. 'There was a lot of beer consumed.'

Maurice had never sailed a wherry before *Hathor* came to Martham, but the information he had gained as a boy, watching the wherries pass Woods' yard as he worked, was sufficient to enable him to take the 56 foot wherry, with a draught of 4 feet and a beam of 14 foot 2 inches, sail area 1175 square feet, along the river without mishap.

Asked what training he had taken to enable him to design boats, Maurice replied, 'I had an eye for design; it's something you have or don't have.'

After forty years successful trading and considerable expansion of the Martham site, Jimmy learnt that he had cancer. He was pushed to his last directors' meeting in a wheel-chair. Soon after his death the business started on a downward path due mainly to the rapid growth of glass-fibre boats. Luckily Cyril's interest in photo-

**Norfolk boats and 'extras' in the film
'Conflict of Wings' 1983**

*The film starred John Gregson and Muriel Pavlow and told the story
of a battle to save a bird sanctuary from being made into a rocket
range by the R.A.F.*

graphy, nurtured at school, enabled him to capture with a simple box camera (a Kodak 66) many unique pictures of his father's designs and of the Broadland scene of his childhood.

The boat yard was handed over to Jimmy and Phyllis Brown's son-in-law, Gordon Curtis and his two sons, Ian and Patrick. Gordon Curtis sold off some of the firm's boats and they can still be seen on many rivers, including the Thames. 'Sadly some are rotting in the field now,' said Maurice, his face clouding at the memory, 'but I suppose that is progress'. His son said gently, 'You, Dad, had the best days, you saw the end of the traditional Broads wooden boats.'

Looking round their comfortable, beautifully-kept bungalow, full of photographs of the past, and seeing the care Cyril took of his father, I stepped outside, back into the late 1990s with real regret.

Janice, a class motor cruiser designed by Maurice Davey

Jimmy and Phyllis Brown

Earlier this century the Norfolk broads spawned many boat yards. Several became very well known: Herbert Woods of Potter Heigham, John Loynes of Wroxham, Jack Powles International of Wroxham, Brooms of Brundall, Richardsons of Stalham and Landamores of Wroxham come immediately to mind, their contributions to the boating industry have been well documented. I wanted to discover the trials, tribulations, and satisfactions in setting up and running a lesser-known boat yard, and so selected one I had sailed past many times in *Wanderbug,* but had never visited.

At one time Martham Boat-building and Development Co. was reputed to be the third largest boat yard in Broadland. It was widely known as 'Brown's yard'.

On a wet, grey winter day, Mrs Phyllis Brown welcomed me into her cosy retirement bungalow on the outskirts of Martham. She told me how her husband, a boat builder, started the yard in 1946, and remained managing director of the yard for thirty-five years. Originally the chairman of the firm was the late Mr Pritchard who had a shed and three sailing cruisers, which was his contribution to the yard's finances. Jimmy's contribution was as a boat-builder who operated day launches from the back yard of his house in the village. Martham was a short distance from the river frontage. Very quickly, the yard was organized; Mr Davey, Mr Wright, and Mr Skoyles became directors and the company was set up.

Phyllis Brown, always interested in people, ran a guest house from their home at Conyard Villa, Martham. She enjoyed life 'working up' the yard. 'There was something about the yard,' she said and her face reflected the happy times of those early years. She also had 'Nan', her mother-in-law, to care for. She lived into her hundred-and-third year.

The *Judith* motor cruisers, a fleet of nine, were named after a neighbour who lived to be one hundred and five. They were identical to their predecessors, the *Janet* class, which grew into a fleet of eight cruisers. When Nan died, Mrs Brown decided to run

Judith IV - the class was named after a neighbour who lived to be 105

a grocery shop for the yard. 'We stocked everything, down to hairpins, as well as groceries for the boats.'

The development of the yard was rapid; in its heyday, the 1960s and 70s, the four directors had a fleet of one hundred boats for hire. Customers came on holiday by train. There was a rail-link from the Midlands, and coach and car transported them to the boats moored up on the river, nearly opposite Candle Dyke. In 1959, the local Midland and Great Northern railway line serving the area closed down; a less convenient but frequent bus and coach service was substituted, and run by the Eastern Counties Omnibus Company. For those customers whose rail terminus was Norwich, the journey could be completed by car, whilst customers from the Manchester and Rochdale areas could travel to Norfolk on an overnight coach and be picked up by a free car service to Martham, from either Potter Heigham Bridge, Acle station or Rollesby. Cars also became much more widely used by private individuals.

Mrs Brown did all the boat laundry in her home, as did the other directors' wives in their homes. They also sewed all the boat curtains and covers. At the end of each season, the four directors' wives shared out the blankets, seven hundred; all had to be washed, dried and aired. Mrs Brown only stopped the blanket wash this year. 'I missed it,' she said.

The rail bridge at Potter Heigham

In the early days, the yard had no telephone on site. The Browns' daughter earned her pocket money by cycling from their home in the village down to the yard - 3d per trip. There was no water on the site, and all boats had to be supplied with drinking water, so a water lorry with a large tank transported water from the Browns' home to fill the boats every Friday evening. There were no petrol pumps at the yard, so fuel was taken there in cans.

Broads visitors who preferred to stay ashore and day-sail were catered for at the Browns' home, in Conyard Villa. They paid seven pounds a week, which included two cooked meals as well as a packed lunch daily. Fresh fruit and vegetables were supplied from nearby farms and a smallholding. Fishing parties were also well catered for, as their catalogue illustrates. During the season, Mrs Brown, with her two helpers, provided full board for an average of twenty guests each week. Coarse fishing extended the season.

Then the war came and all these activities stopped. In fact, when war broke out, the last boat to be built still had to be paid for, and there were no hirings to bring in the money. All cash-flow stopped. By careful budgeting, and frugal living, the debts were gradually settled, and the wood for the boat and its engine were paid for.

During the years of the Second World War, Jimmy Brown went to work at Woods' and Neaves' yards. After the war, development of the yard continued apace. The building of reception hall, dining-room, ballroom and chalets progressed. Greenhouses and a smallholding helped to provide fresh vegetables to sell in the shop and to customers in passing boats.

'Browns' Yard' at Martham

Then the directors wanted to buy a redundant aircraft hangar so that the work on boats could be done in sheltered conditions, but they could not afford the price. However, during the war years, unbeknown to her husband, Mrs Brown had been buying National Saving Certificates. The sum of one hundred and five pounds had accrued. Mrs Brown produced the savings and the hangar was bought. The directors worked all night erecting it. 'What did your husband say when you produced your savings?' I asked. 'Nothing,' she replied, with a happy smile. 'You know what men are, but I saw his chin tremble.'

At work in the shelter of the hangar

Sixteen-footers lined up in the workshop

So full boat production after the war resulted in twenty woman boat-cleaners and thirty boat maintenance staff being employed. The greenhouses, smallholding and flower beds along the river frontage always caught my eye when I sailed past that stretch of the river. I was always curious that somebody had the time and love of the place to grow such beautiful roses in beds by the riverside. It has taken me thirty years to learn the answer (and I confess to going ashore one lovely night to pick a rose for my dinghy. As I made supper and erected my boat tent, the rose smelt sweetly as I curled up in my sleeping bag content after just another day in *Wanderbug.*)

At the yard the days of boat hire of the 50s to the 70s were creative and active. Often Mr Brown would go home after a long day at the yard, and say to his wife, 'Do you feel like sleeping afloat tonight?' or he would return home at the start of the season saying, 'We've launched a boat today, do you want to sleep in her?' So food, blankets and a hot water bottle were collected, the cat provided with fresh milk, and the night would be spent on the river, even if it was a frosty night in February, with ice on the insides of the windows.

The cleaning ladies

'The other directors thought us mad,' said Mrs Brown, 'but we'd had a lovely night - it's another world on the Broads.'

Jimmy's dream to own a wherry materialised in the 1950's when *Hathor* was bought. *Bramble* was also bought for the yard. They were refitted and restored in 1958. Moored in the dyke, *Hathor* and *Bramble* were rented out as houseboats. Often the Browns and ancient Nan lived for days at a time aboard the wherry. 'We just liked being afloat,' said Phyllis. *Hathor,* bought from the Hamilton family, was used by the partners. They took the workmen out for a day's sailing. The men would take a packed lunch, but a hot evening meal was enjoyed at a riverside pub where *Hathor* was moored overnight. Sometimes, trying to get under Potter Heigham bridge, members of the public, who always lined the bridge to watch the proceedings, would be taken aboard the wherry, to act as human ballast. If the wherry was weighed down sufficiently, it was easier to pass through the tiny medieval arch. 'We once sailed *Hathor* to Acle and across Breydon in a thunderstorm,' recalled Mrs Brown.

Bramble sank in the Martham dyke one bad winter. *Hathor* was sold to Peter Bower in 1987 and, after extensive restoration, is now part of the Wherry Yacht Charter Company.

By the late 1970s the Broads holiday trade had started to decline. Caravan holidays, cheap flights abroad and a desire to have luxuries in the boats, such as T.V., heating and hot water, made the business of running a boat yard uneconomic. Wages escalated,

Aboard the *Hathor* - Jimmy Brown second from right

luxury boats cost more to build and service, and the older boats were more difficult to rent out.

Mr Brown retired in 1975, due to ill health. He died of cancer two years later, and when Phyllis Brown, who had been honorary chairman, decided to retire aged seventy, Maurice Davey and Mr Skoyles also retired.

Gordon Curtis came to the boat yard at Martham in 1952 as a boat-builder. He married Jimmy and Phyllis Brown's daughter and took over the running of the boat yard in the 1980s. He and his two sons, Ian and Patrick, now run the yard at a time of great change and competition. Having sold off some of the wooden boats, Gordon concentrated on running a hire fleet with the remainder.

Recently, quite by chance, travelling home after a day's sailing with a friend in that area we drove past Conyard Villa and saw a field full of wooden boats, greenhouses, sheds and trailers beside the roadway. Instantly I remembered all that Mrs Brown had told me about the building up of the company.

In great excitement I went into the main shed and explained my interest in the site and its present occupation. Although I was a total stranger to him, Gordon welcomed me and showed me around the yard. His enthusiasm was infectious and, as we walked over the sawdust floor of the large hangar, old, historic, wooden boats, chocked up in orderly aisles, were shown to me. Craftsmen were sitting in some boats, intent on their repairs, whilst others sat beneath a pall of dust, awaiting their turn. Years rolled by as I recognised names of yachts I had sailed past more than twenty years ago. It was like meeting up with old friends.

Lowering *Hathor*'s mast

Interestingly, boat owners from far away were now allowed to rent off part of the sheds to carry out their own renovation work on their private yachts and cruisers. 'There are not many places on the Norfolk Broads where you can do this,' commented a man from Birmingham who was working on his own yacht and travelled down many weekends to enjoy his hobby.

Another interesting line Gordon and his sons developed was boat trading with Holland, buying and selling boats for private owners. Indeed, only a few days prior to my meeting with Gordon I had sailed past the riverside at Martham and noticed a new, beautifully-built yacht of Dutch design. I was told it was being sailed by her owners towards the south coast at the end of the month.

'We can't stand another bad season,' commented a member of Gordon's staff, and I knew that a line of well-maintained yachts and cruisers lay off the quay-heading at Martham awaiting customers. Everybody was hoping for a good season.

Gordon generously lent me his collection of photographs, and they swept away the years and memories of Maurice Davey's designs, *Janet*, *Janice* and *Japonica* cam back to life.

Walking away from the boat yard where all the men seemed to enjoy their work and to radiate enthusiasm, I saw one or two boats that lay in the field, timbers blackened with age and seams opened by adverse weather. They had had their time and now, like old men, could only dream of the past.

Hathor on quiet waters.

40

Jack Leveridge

I first met Jack at the Museum of the Broads. He was cheerful and enthusiastic about his project to restore *The Yare*, a river commissioner's launch that had been moored near Colman's in the 1930s. Purely by chance he met the museum's creator, Robert Paul, when visiting the museum in its first year. Discovering Jack's background, Robert invited him to become involved in the museum's restoration projects. Jack, now aged eighty-four years, is an active worker for the museum. He was very recently involved in the mammoth task of moving the museum's treasures from the Herbert Woods sheds at Potter Heigham to their new home at Stalham.

At my last visit to Jack's home in Horning, he showed me a rowing dinghy he had just completed for his granddaughter, and his winter job was a partially completed 26-inch model of a wherry.

Jack was born in Kilkenny, Ireland, son of a blacksmith, who served in the First World War as an Army Veterinary sergeant. He sent Jack and his brother and his wife to live with their grandparents in Smallburgh whilst he served his country in France. After the war the family moved to Hoveton. Jack went to the local school, leaving when fourteen, and began work as an apprentice boat builder in H. C. Banham's yard, Horning, in 1928. He worked first with Fred Pitchers, who was a carpenter, doing repairs on boats and also working on buildings. When working on a garage, on the road opposite the yard, they demolished a bank in preparation for building a concrete wall. They found that the bank was full of seashells, which gave credit to the earlier theory that the Broads were formed as a result of a sea surge.

Those early work days were hard. Jack remembers the water flooding into the workshop during the long winters, with only a cast-iron stove in one corner of the workshop for heat. His wage was 6s.6d per week, and he was expected to buy his own woodworking tools. After five years as an apprentice, Jack had two years to serve as an improver. When qualified, he earned 2s. 4d an hour.

At fifteen Jack was sent out to sail with Nat Bircham, and he remembers learning to quant as they sailed from Potter Heigham to Horning, and also how to shoot bridges. 'Nat used to sail right up to a bridge,' remembered Jack. 'Once the main was down, the mast and jib came down together, right at the last moment. I only made a mess of it once, and that was when a block jammed.'

Another early highlight in Jack's career was when he went on a motor launch with a friend, Jack Edwards, on a motor launch called *Towyou*, running trips on Barton Broad from the staithe to the island on regatta days. At that time there were seven wherries sailing, and when Jack and his friend returned to the yard after a long day afloat, the yard manager and foreman were waiting, telling them they must return a yacht to Wroxham, as the people on board had to return home urgently. They were provided with a lantern for use on the foredeck of the yacht, and it was 11.00 p.m. before the fifteen-year-old boy completed his day's work. Other sailing experiences included taking customers out for an hour's drive on such launches as *Wildfire*, *Joyce* and *Night Rider*.

Banham's yard built a number of hire launches and also some yachts whilst Jack served his apprenticeship with them. He particularly enjoyed building in wood. The well-known pleasure wherry *Rambler* gave Jack this experience, as he was given the job of fitting new floorboards in her. The biggest vessel built at that time was the forty-two-foot Monarch class. Banham's was the first yard to build baths in their cruisers, 'little cast-iron things,' said Jack. Theirs was also the first yard to give paid holidays to their staff.

During the Horning regatta, Jack and other apprentices were offered local boats so that they could compete in the boatmans' race as crew, but other jobs allotted to them were not so enjoyable, and Jack remembers having to dig a hole under the keel of *White Rose*, so that a new bolt could be fitted. Another job Jack had to do also involved *White Rose*. The foreman boat-builder, Harry, fell out with the other boat-builder, Reggie, whilst Jack, as apprentice, had to help both men. For two weeks he had to go from one man to the other. Harry would ask Jack, 'What's the young bugger up to now?' Going back to Reggie he would be asked, 'What's the old bugger up to now?'

Another of Jack's yarns was that when he moored the *White Rose* up for lunch, he used to drop a line over the side weighted with a piece of fat meat to catch an eel. His holiday people saw him to this and asked what it was for and he told them. He was asked if he would catch one for them the next day. A large eel was caught and when he opened it, it was full of a big tad, so he washed it well and cooked it for them, and when he asked them what they thought of it, they said it was lovely.

A wherry mast was situated outside the workshop to facilitate the lifting out of engines, and also small craft. A bosun's chair was fitted, and once, Jack remembers being hoisted up to return a newly-painted weather vane to the top of the wherry mast. The yard bell went to summons the men to their 'elevenses', and in their haste to get to their drinks, they forgot to lower Jack, and there he swung until the tea break was over.

As a boy Jack recalls the very hard winters when the river froze over and there were deep snow drifts. Many moorhens froze to death, and once a bittern was heard calling; on investigation, the bird was found to have a broken beak. The water then was quite clear, and he used it to boil to make tea for the men in the yard.

Jack remained at Banham's at Horning for thirty-two years, until H. C. Banham died in 1960; by then Percival's Boats had amalgamated with Banham's. The yard was sold and Jack went to work at Porter and Haylet's at Wroxham. During his fourteen years with this yard, he recalls working on the yacht *Rose Rambler*, owned by the late Humphrey Barton who made fourteen Atlantic crossings in her.

In the 1960s, the birth of the *Peter Duck* came about because

Ernie Porter had heard about the original sea-going yacht. He took Jack with him to inspect the boat, and it was decided it needed to be updated. The designer, Laurence Giles, was given the job, and Jack helped complete the boat and get it ready to put on show at the London Boat Show. Subsequently Jack sea-trialled all the thirty-four Peter Duck boats. They were all built at Porter and Haylets, launched and motored to Yarmouth and out to sea.

The launch of the *Peter Duck*

'I went out on sea trials with the first boat,' said Jack, 'and it went to Canada, but the most interesting trip was when we were caught in a gale. At that time we had a Trinity House Pilot with us and we found the sea began to break over us and we had a job to shorten the sail; even then we were surging down the waves at 10 knots. The hull was built for a speed of 6 knots! We managed to put in by Felixstowe and crossed over and went up the Twizzle, then Fred and I got in the pram dinghy with outboard and went on to the Club House at Walton-on-the-Naze. On the way we spotted an outboard motor lying in the mud so we took it to the club where

OUTLINE SPECIFICATION

CONSTRUCTION IS TO LLOYD'S REGISTER OF SHIPPING REQUIREMENTS FOR CLASSIFICATION 100A1 YACHT

PLANKING:	Iroko hardwood ⅞" finished thickness.	HATCHES:	Mahogany laminae, canvas covered.
TIMBERS:	English Oak	BULKHEADS:	15 m.m. marine ply.
		DECK:	15 m.m. marine ply, canvas covered.
FLOORS:	English Oak, galvanised iron as required.	SPARS:	Masts hollow Spruce, booms Spruce.
FASTENINGS:	Generally copper and rooved. Gun metal hood-ends and garboards. Galv. steel bolts as necessary.	RIGGING:	Galvanised F.S.W.R. and hemp.
STEM: STERNPOST: KEEL: DEADWOODS:	Iroko.	MAST TABERNACLE AND FITTINGS: PULPIT, STERN- GUARD, STANCHIONS:	Galvanised steel.
SHELVES: STRINGERS:	English Oak or Larch	BALLAST KEEL:	Cast iron 38 cwt.
COAMINGS: CABIN TRUNKING:	Iroko or Mahogany.	PAINTING:	Topsides 5 coats, bottom 5 coats including anti-fouling.
CABIN TOP:	Laminated ply, no beams, canvas covered.		Brightwork 4 coats best yacht varnish.
		TANKS:	Fuel 25 gallons. Water 25 gallons.
		LIGHTING:	12 volts.

ENGINE : NEWAGE-B.M.C. 1.5 litre " Captain " diesel, 4 cylinders,
electric starting, fresh water cooled by Heat Exchanger.

This engine develops a maximum continuous power of 31 b.h.p. at 3,000 r.p.m. though in the PETER DUCK the revolutions are kept to approximately 2,000 r.p.m. This is more than adequate for the hull, and will give a speed of about 7 knots. 2:1 reduction gearing is fitted and drive to the central 3-bladed propeller is by stainless steel shaft with cutless rubber outboard bearing.

ACCOMMODATION

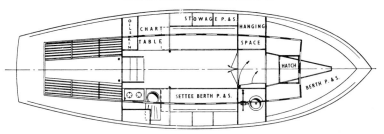

There is 6' headroom in fore cabin and saloon, with 6' 6" under the doghouse.

The fore-cabin has two full length berths with stowage below. Folding door to W.C. compartment (can also be used to shut off the W.C. itself). To port there is capacious space for hanging clothes and stowage of gear. Double doors lead to the saloon with settee berths either side with padded backrests and stowages outboard. Folding table fitted amidships. The full size chart table is to port as is the oilskin locker. Galley to starboard with stainless steel sink and 2 burner cooker. There is generous space for stowage of crockery, cooking utensils and stores. Companion ladder and sliding hatch give access to self-draining cockpit with seats and exceptionally large lockers giving much more than ample space for stowage of bosun's stores and sails.

Outline specification for the Peter Duck Class 'close to the ideal for the cruising yachtsman'.

we then found that two young men went to check on their boat and had got lost in the wind and one stuck in the mud. The outboard had to be rescued and one of the boys taken to hospital. We were well looked after at the Club House.

Peter Duck approaching Wroxham Bridge

I sailed out of Yarmouth with an owner, who looked ahead at the bar; it was a bit rough but I got him to sail through it. On our return, he was very happy and said I had given him great confidence in the handling of the boat.

We also built a twin-engined motor cruiser for a local owner. I went on sea trials with him and also spent a few days on board with him and his friends. We put into Ostend, then went on to Rotterdam; from there we did a spot of fishing with a spinner and caught a number of mackerel until the owner said "This is not a bloody fishing boat!" We had no volunteer to clean and cook the fish so we gave them all away.'

During World War II Jack hoped to join the R.A.F., but being in a reserved occupation as shipwright he was not accepted. He helped at Percival's Yard working on the Motor Landing Craft and torpedo boats. After the war, he returned to his old yard. In 1974

Jack went to a boat yard in Brundall, specifically to fit out a yacht for designer John Bennett; however, when that was completed, he stayed on doing other work. During this time he got his first order to fit alloy windows and in 1975 he started his own business, Trend Marine Products, which manufactured these products. Jack retired in 1980, and the business, now operating from Catfield, continues to be run by his two sons, employing nearly one hundred staff.

Now over eighty years old, Jack enjoys a very active retirement with his wife Eileen, whom he married in 1934. His keen sense of humour is illustrated in the following two stories:-

'We had to wait for some timber to be delivered, so myself and the other apprentice had to caulk the bottom of the boat. The two painters had to paint the bottom inside; they laughed at us crawling under. However, we saw where the paint tins stood and gave a good bang under and upset the paint. We both made off and came back later, one after the other. I was caught and was put up on my bench and my forehead varnished and sawdust was about to be added, so. I picked up the dolly and went through the window which saved me from a worse fate.

While a skipper's mate with one of the men from Banham yard, I was moored near St Olaves and had to cook a chicken, potatoes and greens. We had a two-burner paraffin stove, one small tin oven and one primus stove. With everything cooking, we heard somebody walking along the deck and a member of the company called the skipper and said "Could you do this Yorkshire pudding for us?" The skipper looked up and said "What do you think this is? A bloody restaurant?" '

Jack's retirement project, a boat for his grandchildren.

Sydney Loynes

I met Sydney at the A.G.M. of the Museum of the Broads in 1997. As the crowds circulated around the fascinating collection of Norfolk's boating history, in one of Herbert Woods' boat sheds at Potter Heigham, I confided to Syd my interest in collecting parts of Norfolk's water-borne past through the experiences of people. 'Can we have a mardle sometime about the good old days?' I ventured. He agreed with enthusiasm. 'Of course gal, but you'll have to wait until I return from my honeymoon.' Then that tall, lean, octogenarian called over his new wife, Erica. The fondness they had for one another was plain to see, and I looked forward to meeting them both on their return from a world cruise, which was a 'lovely historic cruise on *Black Prince*,' as Erica reported later. They had met in 1994 on a Saga holiday based at Plymouth. Later Mrs Erica Spickett, a widow, came from her home in Kent to look after Sydney as a friend. They found they shared the same interests, and had the same sense of humour, so when Syd had a heart attack, Erica's visits to Norfolk became more prolonged, and she sold her house in Kent. Together they shared a happy year in Syd's retirement home in Sheringham.

Sadly, I never met Sydney again, as he was taken to hospital. However, he was so keen to record his memories for me that he and Erica made many notes at his hospital bed. One touching letter from her explained that she would jot down notes at the bedside, and later type them up. 'The final paragraph I am not sure about - poor Sydney was in rather a lot of pain, when he was telling me about the flags this afternoon,' she explained. This letter in February 1998 was followed by one in early April when Erica wrote, 'I am afraid Sydney is very poorly in the Benjamin Court Unit at Cromer, and I cannot hold out any hope that you will be able to meet up to reminisce about the Broads. I have made one or two more notes for you...' Sydney died on April 9th 1998, and since then Erica has helped me record his life.

Sydney Robert Loynes, son of Robert (Bob), was born in Hoveton on September 20th 1915. He attended school at Wroxham and, like his father, was a member of the Wroxham Church choir from a young age until he left home to join the Merchant Navy as a lad of fourteen years. Mrs Loynes played the church organ, and young Sydney had to pump the organ for his mother. She must have enjoyed music because she said how much she looked forward to the pianos (all three of them) when they were brought home from the Loynes' hire fleet boats to spend the winter in their house.

Sydney was an active, adventurous lad who would often swim home instead of walking. His clothes were given to Cora, his sister, as he left the primary school, and he would swim to the bridge before collecting his clothes. Playing around his father's boat yard, with his cousin 'Prosser' (John), gave the boys much opportunity to learn about boats. There was also opportunity to earn pocket money in various ways. The village boys who walked to church on Sunday mornings to sing in the choir would invariably meet the cattle which had been driven from Norwich Cattle Market the previous day to their new homes on the farms in the Wroxham and Hoveton area. 'We would stand in the gateways of the houses in Upper Wroxham to stop the cattle getting into people's gardens,' said Sydney. The river at Wroxham Bridge was the first stopping place for watering and resting the animals. On the upside bank of the river, on the Hoveton side, was an area of grass and shallow water and sand, and the cattle would be allowed to drink and rest until the local farmers arrived with their own drovers to take the cattle to their farms. The professional drovers would then be paid off and they would make their own way back to Norwich. 'We were more hindrance than help to the drovers,' remembered Sydney, 'and we must have stank of cows as we donned surplices on arrival at church.' Small shops have now been built on that area by the river bank. A Circus and Fair were held annually on land in Hoveton where Roy's Food Store now stands. At other times, the open land was a suitable site for Sydney and his friends to play football and cricket. In winter, when the marshy ground froze over, skating was the boys' occupation.

A train, referred to as 'Broadland Special', came to Wroxham from London to bring down the holiday makers. They would arrive between 2.00 pm and 3.00 pm on a Saturday. Schoolboys Sydney and John would meet this train with a hand cart and take the luggage to the boat yards to be loaded on to the hire boats. By completing their 'order book' with their prospective clients' names, they made sure they earned extra pocket money when the boats returned to the Loynes' yard the following Saturday. The luggage was re-loaded back on to the hand carts for the return journey to Wroxham station.

Mooring the *Queen of the Broads* was another job that earned the boys an extra one penny. This was a steamer which came from Yarmouth with day trippers. When approaching Acle bridge, if the tide was fairly high, say half flood or more, the *Queen* would increase speed to dig herself deeper in the water, and with funnel lowered, she would just clear the bridge. Staying at Wroxham for about two hours, passengers could have lunch ashore, or look around Roy's before returning to Yarmouth.

'Uncle Ted's Shed' was a store to house the hire fleets' crockery and linen. Also from here, Uncle Ted used to hire out skiffs. Rowing was a popular pastime with many people before the increase in large motor cruises which saw the end of the rowing boat era. Young Sydney would clean the primus stoves in Uncle Ted's shed. More pocket money.

Possibly Sydney's memories went back to his happy childhood in his last days. He took great pains to ask Erica to explain to me the significance of the flags which always flew from an early Roy's Food Store. Apparently there were always four flags on the Stalham road side of the buildings, and a Union Jack flag facing the village street corner and a further four flags facing Church Road. These flags were spelling out 'ROY'S' using the International signalling code. The flags are depicted in the Loynes catalogue, now stored in the Museum of the Broads.

Sydney left school at fourteen years and, not wanting to join the family business, joined the Merchant Navy. During the war, carrying supplies of food from U.S.A. to U.K., he was torpedoed, three times. On the third occasion the men, in a lifeboat, watched the German U-boat surface close by. Expecting to be gunned down, the British survivors watched as the German captain saluted the men before passing over to them food, water and a first-aid kit. Sydney was taken to America after being rescued. Whilst awaiting a boat to get him back to England, he supported himself by washing up in a restaurant. 'It was a way of eating,' he said.

Invalided out of the Merchant Navy, Sydney trained as a

technical librarian in High Wycombe. He established a library for the paper industry, and some time later was sent out to South Africa to establish a similar one there. He and his Norfolk-born wife Freda (whose grandfather, Alfred Pegg, had a boat yard comprising one shed and an office, off Church Road, Hoveton) enjoyed their life in South Africa. During this time, Sydney travelled to U.S.A., Australia, Mexico and Brazil, reading papers on the technical aspect of paper production. On reaching retirement, he and Freda returned to Norfolk, setting up home at Dilham where Sydney kept a boat on the canal. Freda's health had always been poor; they had no children, and, after their marriage was dissolved, Sydney moved to Sheringham, where he enjoyed an active retirement, playing bowls and enjoying Country and Western music.

Sydney's love of boats continued all his life. His last sail was with John Knight in *Gypsy* (built by Alfred Pegg, Freda's grandfather). A lover of all Broadland topics, Sydney was a frequent correspondent with people who owned boats and he often used local papers to write about his interests. In one letter an 80-year-old Miss Jean Metcalf, grandchild of Arthur Pegg, wrote:- (4/8/95) 'I seem to

Sydney Loynes' last trip in *Gypsy*

51

remember names of Pegg-built boats; *Gypsy, Waif, Stray, Nomad, Vagabond, Leisure Hour* - I wonder if the blue pennant with a white "p" is still flying? Actually I noticed your opening sentence, and wondered whether the "rare bird of the Broads" you mentioned alluded to my wonderful grandfather's large entrance hall lined with glass cases of stuffed birds and small animals in their natural habitat. He was such a lovely loving grandfather, and we all enjoyed our stays in "Fir Dene", and the many interesting walks with him - he knew everything about Nature.'

Another letter from Jean (21. 9. 96) says 'It was extremely kind of you to refer the details to me, - in order to furnish details of *Prudence* our boat...Mary Upton now lives at Coldham, Surlingham, enthusiastic sailors all, - her husband John owns Pegg's *Vagabond* built in 1922. They were the senders of your newspaper appeal, thereby beginning our correspondence...'

After Sydney's death there were many generous bequests, some benefactors being the Albion Wherry Trust, Hunter's Yard, R.N.L.I., Salvation Army, British Legion, Redwing Horse Sanctuary, with a request that the money be used in local charities if possible. The family boat-building tool box and many pictorial records of the Loynes boat yard have been loaned by Erica to the Museum of the Broads.

Sydney's grandfather, John Loynes, born in Woodton, between Norwich and Bungay, was the founder of the Loynes boat-building

John Loynes, pioneer of Broadland hire fleets

and hire fleet business. As boy he started work at fourteen years as a house-boy on a large estate at Brooke Hall. There was a large lake in the hall grounds and John, interested in building model yachts, was allowed to sail them on the lake. His next employment was as a carpenter's apprentice at Bungay. After serving his time, he left to work in London, but rejected city life and returned to Norwich, where he set up in Elm Hill as a master carpenter. In his spare time he would go boating on the River Wensum. He found local boats too heavy to drag over the weirs on the Back river, so he built himself a lighter boat. In this he voyaged far along Broadland rivers. Later he built a bigger boat, fully rigged with a cutter sail, capable of making passages over Breydon.

By then a small boat-hire business was established in Elm Hill, but this was not a natural site as customers had to return to base nightly. So John took a boat on a handcart and walked it to Wroxham to start exploring the Northern rivers. Two friends asked to rent his boat, and so began his boat-hire business in 1878. In 1880 a model fishing boat for the Norfolk waters gained John a bronze medal at the National Fisheries Exhibition in Norwich. The following year he was awarded first prize at Great Yarmouth, and in 1883 came a gold medal at the International Fisheries Exhibition in London. So a boat-designer at Wood's turned his dream of setting up his own business (albeit with no capital) into reality. Boats were built of increasing size and sophistication, from the simple camping dinghy with a canvas weather-proof overnight shelter, to a fleet of cabin yachts from three to fifteen tons. George Christopher Davies, writing about the Loyne hire fleet boats, said they were 'beamy, of light draught, with centre-boards and one sail, Una fashion, with a collapsible cabin roof.'

Time to relax aboard the yacht _Coral_

In the Diamond Jubilee year of 1897, John Loyne established a similar holiday yachting business on the Friesland Meres in Holland, and two of his largest yachts *Victoria* and *Enterprise* were sailed across the Channel where they spent several years being hired out before the decline of business due to anti-British feelings during the Boer War. In the 1890s the Norfolk Broads Yachting Company, an agency for hiring out boats was established with bases at Wroxham and Potter Heigham.

After the Armistice in 1918 trading wherries were converted into pleasure craft. John Loynes bought the old Caister Lifeboat *Caister Maid* to convert her into an eight-berth yacht. Later he copied this conversion and built the *Golden Hind*, a very popular letting craft.

Aboard the *Golden Hind*

The Second World War brought closure of the Loynes yard, but John died shortly before the outbreak of hostilities, eighty-three years after he had first started work. He died in 1939, aged ninety-six years.

When the war ended in 1945 the business was re-started with Sydney Loynes and three outside directors. Later, a fifth member of the family, another John Loynes, joined them. The firm carried on until 1959, when it was taken over by Mr Norman Adams of St Olaves.

In 1982, the *Eastern Daily Press* newspaper reported 'Loynes Wroxham Boat Yard is sold. Eleven men are made redundant. Loynes celebrated its century in 1978, and the pioneer yard, started with a fourteen foot rowing boat and a shed on Monastery Staithe off Elm Hill, has been bought by Mr Len Funnell who will continue the business.'

J. Loynes & Sons Ltd. in its centenary year, 1978

Billy May and Family

Sailing around Broadland collecting stories from boatmen with long and loving memories is always fascinating; it is usually the passion of the person that compels me to listen. On a gloomy, dank day in early February I went to visit Harry and Celia May who, with their sons Alan and James, run Maycraft boat yard. They were committed to their lifestyle, but it was the boat shed where we met that charmed me. It was in a time warp.

Walking along a muddy lane beside the river Thurne and the fringing riverside bungalows, with the long, low lines of flooded marshes, fringed by golden reeds stretching westwards as far as the eye could see; it was a world away from the warm offices of Herbert Woods where I was given directions to get to Maycraft boat yard.

We stood in a riverside shed, surrounded by boats in various stages of repair, and Harry told me about his father, Billy May. He was the son of a schoolmaster, born in Edgefield School House near Holt, in 1920. He learnt to sail at Burnham Overy, and was apprenticed as boat-builder at Herbert Woods' Yard. Over the years he earned a reputation for winning races at all the local sailing regattas in a clinker built boat *Kestrel*, a two-berth sailing cruiser about twenty-one feet in length, with a tall Bermudian mast. The boat went well in a light breeze and beat everything in sight, said his son.

During the war years Billy was occupied building torpedo boats and air-sea rescue launches, but in the 1950s left Woods' Yard to set up his own company which he called Maycraft.

Billy built a small fleet of motor launches. Often fishermen rented them, and also families hired the riverside bungalows. He was amongst the earliest members of the Broadland Association; also he was a founder member of the Lady Yacht Club, holding regattas for the Lady yachts built at the Woods' yard after the second world war. He died at the age of seventy-four in 1994. Denis Kirkham, colleague and friend of Billy's for nearly half a century, said, 'He was a first-class racing helm, always with a smile, usually with a pipe and often a drink. He had a Norfolk charm of a type that is fast fading.'

Harry May and son in the Maycraft boat shed

Possibly Billy will be remembered best for the Cromer crab boats that he built in his yard at Potter Heigham. One is an exhibition feature at the Cromer Boat Museum, and many of these boats working from Sheringham and Cromer were built at his yard. Crab boats, clinker-built, double-ended, broad-beamed, even tubby; always oak for keel stem and stern posts with oak ribs. Arruck holes, two-a-side, were cut so that oars could be used if the engine failed. Pulling such heavy work boats up a stony beach, possibly through surf, would have taken skilled timing; slipping oars through the arruck holes enabled the fishermen to carry the boats up the beach. The crab boats' special shape enabled them to lift forward throwing water clear, and handle reliably in rough seas so that the crew could work the pots.

Crab boat on Cromer Beach

Since a lot of tide and surf runs along the Norfolk coast, when the crab boats surfed into a beach and touched bottom, they came round into the waves and would lie over. As the men sat on the side of the boat, it would be washed up the beach but would not fill up with water.

Billy had five children, and Harry his son (with *his* sons) now continues to trade from Maycraft yard. Harry had his first sail in

Kestrel aged three months. His schooling was at Potter Heigham and Stalham local schools, then he went to work with his father. Whilst his wife, Celia, made us cups of tea, I looked around the shed. Outside, the muddy river flowed downstream and a swan slipped out of it and plodded her webbed way into the boat shed. Whilst we ate sandwiches she went from one to the other accepting titbits from our hands. She was obviously a long-standing visitor. Towards the back of the shed, timbers were stacked across the rafters. Beneath, in various stages of decay or restoration, were three large wooden hulls of yachts. The wind whistled through the unheated shed, fluttering their tarpaulins. Tools were everywhere. I was shown a steam box and steam oven and told how they were used. Later in the day Harry's two boys, James and Alan, gave me demonstration of how they used a dolly, then I watched them 'clinking up', one lad inside the boat hammering down the nails, whilst the other held the metal dolly in position to secure the proper placing of the nails along the boat's hull. I was shown how the edges of the planks were prepared so that cotton caulking would complete the repair. Harry told me that 'clinking up' was costed out at twelve pounds per foot.

Harry showed me a Stuart Turner pump taken out of an old boat, kept to be donated to the Museum of the Broads. Other historic items, planes, chisels, an old sea toilet, brass pumps and nuts, bolts and screws of every size and shape lay in boxes ready to be passed on. 'I throw nothing away,' said Harry. 'I go to the boot sales and buy what other people would call rubbish.' Standing on the sawdust-coated floor of the shed, Harry leaned against a huge block of wood; on closer inspection I saw it was a very beautiful piece of wood. It was the bottom half of the stem post of some very old boat - nobody could remember her name. Memorabilia coated the walls, rafters and floors of this draughty boat shed; it was indeed a very special place - actually, a living, working museum. It reminded me of our trips in America, where we were invited to rest and stay and be part of the boat museum. Along our route off the eastern seaboard from Florida to Chesapeake Bay were places where the nautical past and present fused into a seamless line of time. So it seemed to me in Maycraft's No. 1 shed that day.

Harry talked about the Cromer crab boats. He thought his father probably built about thirty of them. Those and the lifeboats were the only ones that gained Lloyds Register Exemption, because they were built so strong and heavy. Harry went on to explain that the White Fish Authority gave a government loan to the fishermen, who got a third of the cost of their crab boat over a ten year loan. He explained that Billy would first lay the keel of the double-ender, and three ribs along its length. The officials from the ministry would issue money at this stage, then the next stage of planking up was begun and the engine ordered. Timbers were steamed and put into position. Inspectors specified that the scarfing of the planks had to be three feet apart. The top plank was scarfed in the middle, and was hardwood (oak) as was the bottom plank. The garboard, the 'sand struk', needed extra strength, being the spot where the boat would first hit the beach on landing and be pulled over stones and gritty sand by the fishermen. The engine bearers would be put in position next, but the boat could not be painted until the inspectors had checked on the quality of wood used and the workmanship employed.

On a subsequent visit to Maycraft, Harry supplied me with more information on crab boats. It appeared that about fifty crab boats were built at Maycraft over twenty-five years. A drawing of a beach boat exactly like the crabbers was discovered on a map of 1586. The earlier crabbers, rowed and sailed, were slightly smaller than the modern ones. The system of using them has not altered very much however. The crew sail up to their buoy and haul it up, then an anchor is attached to the pots. Crab pots used to have oak frames with four hoops made of hazel or chestnut. This is covered with netting which used to be of manilla, but is now of nylon. There are twenty-five pots to a shank, and each pot is separated by fourteen fathoms of rope. There are six shanks; all used to be hand-hauled. When the catch is removed from the pots and they are re-baited, the boat turns around, and the pots are re-laid.

I also found that Billy and his son built a forty-seater launch, designed to ferry trippers from Morston to Blakeney Point. It was the biggest boat built at Maycraft yard at that time. The Morston Ferry, a twenty-five foot open ferry boat, with hull shape very similar to the crab boats, was sailed by her owner from Potter Heigham via Yarmouth to Morston to start her working life.

The work that Harry specialises in is repair and restoration of old boats. His skills are all the result of his father's training. As a

Billy May in one of his crab boats

boy he remembers walking to school through Woods' yard to pick up a lift, and watching the men sawing the ice with a hacksaw to make water space for the boats when all the sheds were packed full of boats. That was in the big freeze of 1952. Another big freeze-up was the winter of 1962/3. 'A boat was built for a customer in Shed No.1. He wanted it in a hurry, so we dragged the boat over the ice to Shed No.2. We thought it safer to take the boat to the engine rather than the other way round. Seven men were used to drag the boat over the ice. If the ice broke the men were prepared to jump into the boat,' explained Harry. 'The ice was measured nineteen inches thick on the edges of the river and fifteen inches thick in the middle. The men could hear the ice crack and groan with the six to nine inches rise and fall of the tide as the river rushed up and down beneath the ice.'

Harry cares passionately about the old yachts in his care. 'Treat the old girl right,' is his firm advice to his customers, which means checking that the boat is well ventilated, lockers left open and bunks and cupboards kept well aired when the end of the season comes. Once he saw a small boy abusing his dinghy; it belonged to *Prudence*. He took the dinghy from the boy, then rang his father and explained what he had done. Because he is very restricted for workshop space, Harry looks after private boats in the customers' sheds and dykes along their frontage. *Dusky Maiden*, built in the mid-30s with her ten-foot-long dinghy, and *Peanuts* are two such boats, as is *Bobby* and was *Prudence*. Currently the yard is restoring a 1927-built yacht *Viking*. When she was bought by her present owner she was insured for two hundred and fifty pounds. After her restoration, her value will be in the region of many thousands of pounds.

Harry walked me along the river bank from shed No. 1 down river. It was heart-breaking to see the state of some of the boats overwintering along the banks, lawns and dykes; tarpaulins torn in the wind or lying rotting on the blackened, rotting decks. In contrast, in one shed was a beautiful boat, one of Harry's projects. Two years ago, the family owning her said they could not afford the thousands of pounds required for her restoration. Harry rented them a G.R.P. boat for use when they holidayed in their bungalow, after which they told Harry to go ahead and restore their family heirloom.

Walking back to his work bench, Harry pointed out his next project, his own boat. She is *Water Soldier*, a Waveney One Design, No.7, a wooden half-decker. Twenty-six were built, the last being in G.R.P., 'bloody tupperware,' said Harry contemptuously. Sitting in a dejected state in the water, the old lady is in need of care, and Harry, who loves to sail, is looking forward to getting her ready for the coming season. He recalls when Hickling Sailing Club had no club-house, just a lighter tied up against the reeds where the club house now stands, to act as a committee boat.

'Men wanted something to do on Sundays, and they wanted to sail for fun. Alternate meetings were held at Hickling and Thurne. Twenty to thirty boats would regularly turn up, anything from half-deckers to dinghies. Class A was a race consisting of any type of boat as was Class B. "Anything" just had to be under fourteen feet O.A. or over,' explained Harry, grinning broadly at the memories.

Billy May predicted that, in the future, people would need three jobs. That has proved prophetic in the case of his versatile grandsons. Alan and James not only work with their father repairing boats, they also repair and raise up riverside bungalows, building extensions too if required. In addition they act as removers of furniture, being responsible for storing customers belongings and moving items of furniture in and out of people's summer homes. The present Maycraft hire fleet consists of motor launches, some of which were built by their grandfather. All can be hired by the day or week.

Out for the day in a Maycraft motor launch

Alan and James say that they enjoyed growing up around the boat yard. 'Somebody was always about.' They both enjoy working there too 'especially in the winters', and their quiet enthusiasm and zeal for historic craft in their care makes one feel better about the future of Broadland.

Mick Richardson

Mick Richardson was born in Northampton in 1923. Both his grandfathers were successful men, one a business man, the other Deputy Chief Constable of Northampton. Mick's father was an inventor. He discovered the means of extracting iron dust and returning it to the furnace clean. He owned quarries and some of his inventions were concerned with the by-products of steel. He made a fortune but lost it all during the war, as his money had been invested in Germany.

Mick, booked to be educated at Dartmouth Naval College, had those plans revised due to the change in the family fortunes. As an alternative he took up engineering. He worked for the River Nene Catchment Board. After a spell as deputy engineer, he moved to Wisbech where he was responsible for the construction of piling on the river bank and for building the town quay.

During the war years, Mick was an engineer in Burma, after which he returned home to retrain at Loughborough College. At just twenty-seven, he was offered a contract in Hertfordshire, so terminating his college training. He worked for five years on a New Town development, building a link road to establish a traffic route between Letchworth and London.

Mick married in 1950. His wife's parents were from Norfolk although his wife was born in Northampton. For two years he worked as a contract engineer to re-develop open-cast mines in Newcastle. When this firm collapsed, he became assistant engineer at Chertsey, building a tank-testing track to develop an experimental road-building surface. All motorways still use this system today. In 1953 came the east coast floods, and Mick was later put in charge of rebuilding the sea walls at Foulness. His wife had to live in a caravan, travelling around wherever Mick was employed. The couple grew tired of the nomadic family life, and so Mick decided on a change in career. His father-in-law took over the Bridge Hotel at Potter Heigham. Mick was offered the job of running the Broads Haven Club.

The business thrived, and Mick's adaptability stood him in good stead. There was a good relationship with the brewery; then the brewery was taken over and Mick was offered redundancy. 'I should have got out then,' said Mick, 'but I had a family so I stayed on and fought the brewery's decision.' Unfortunately, his father-in-law did not have an agreement with the brewery in writing, so the business was lost.

Looking towards the Bridge Hotel, Potter Heigham

Mick Richardson bought the boat yard upstream of the Bridge Hotel. The yard's shed was in a state of near-collapse, but as an experienced engineer, Mick was able to jack up the shed and concrete the base; but before the yard could be developed, the River Board put a constraint on its development by saying that no construction could take place on the site. With the compensation offered, Mick pulled down his shed, erecting it on another site down-stream. There he concentrated on building up his hire fleet. Soon an eight-berth motor cruiser, *Uncle Remus,* joined the two-berth cruisers such as *Brer Rabbit.* Mick took a partner, John Perryman. 'They were great times,' Mick enthused. 'We knew so many people. I had my last sail with Percy Hunter in the 1960s. We got on well. He died two weeks later.'

Another boat yard, also named Richardson, outgrew its site on Oulton Broad, and in 1957 moved to new premises to Stalham. To avoid confusion with two boat yards with the same name in the same area, Mick renamed his yard, 'Phœnix Fleet.' Meanwhile the business expanded. Nine motor cruisers were designed by Mick. Also the Lady class of motor cruisers from Herbert Woods were bought in to join the Phœnix Fleet. 'I went into boats and had a boat yard because I loved boats,' said Mick. 'Nowadays it is too commercialized. In the old days, money came in because the boats were good and so was the service. Nowadays one only hears about the profits and not the service.'

Possibly Mick's best-remembered design was that of the *Slipstream*. He bought the original half-rater in 1950, and used her as the basis for his future design of this cold-moulded boat. 'That was one you got right,' said Tim Whelpton to Mick some time later. Six *Slipstreams* were built. The original one was towed to Thurne mouth to compete in the local regatta, after which Mick employed a professional skipper and crew to take it around the country to compete in time-trials. The weed-infested Broads impeded the boats' speed, so Mick redesigned her hull shape and rudder to take this problem into account.

Only last summer I saw the *Slipstream* for the very first time. At the end of a beautiful day on Horsey, I was sailing back to Hickling late in the day. Going in the opposite direction an unusual yacht was broad-reaching away from Hickling. I turned and was compelled to look at her rigging and hull until she disappeared around a bend in the river. She glided along in the merest breath of wind, and was a most elegant shape. Later, I found out that Mick's daughter and her husband had been on holiday, based at Hickling, using their father's *Slipstream;* when I passed them, I assume they were on their way back to the Phœnix yard.

Mick is president of the Lady class, and he still retains chairmanship of the Phœnix Fleet yard. His retirement hobbies are wide-ranging. His knowledge of French wines is considerable, and in his garden, he is experimenting with growing various vines. His conservatory also is full of growing vines. Mick is also a skilled water-colourist. 'I found I could paint after fifty years,' he commented, as he showed me his sketch book. In addition, Mick cooks well, possibly a skill learnt whilst he worked at Broads Haven Club. After I had enjoyed sharing supper with him, we listened to some of his CDs. He has an extensive collection, and a delight in choral music.

***Slipstream*, winner of the 'Three Rivers Race' in 1993
Designed by Mick Richardson, based on the Thames Rater**

Mick's two sons now run the boat yard at Potter Heigham. They have a fleet of launches that can be hired out for the day or week. They also specialize in pilotage through the historic bridge at Potter, and Phœnix Fleet yard is ideally situated to carry out this work during the summer. Both Robin and Patrick sail competitively, owning white boats which they race at Wroxham. Also they race cruisers, and I was thrilled to be shown their beautifully-cared-for yachts, still under their winter wraps: *Firebird,* a Bermudian-rigged yacht launched in 1996, whilst beside her lay his brother's *Buttercup,* built by Ernest Collins, and launched in 1896, exactly one hundred years and one month earlier.

Although I arrived at the yard without an appointment, this friendly company showed me round, and they had every right to be proud of their yard. Inside one shed, the oldest two-storey boat shed on the broads, *Zingara,* built in 1894, was being restored. Whilst Sid Wren, a well-known boat man of the Herbert Woods era, was busy on it, her owner turned up to visit. Quite a personal touch

In the adjoining shed were seven yachts, all in private hands, and in a quite beautiful state, with varnish gleaming, and wood-warm hulls ready for spring launch, now only weeks away. In another shed I was shown another line of water-waiting historic yachts; one a Yare Bure No. 6, built in 1910, was especially eye-catching. Here also, *Flight,* a 1918 yacht, had been rebuilt. 'How do you get this work?' I asked. 'Personal recommendation,' was the simple reply. Robin went on to comment that there were still many good boat-builders on the Broads, but many did not get the opportunity to work on the kind of yachts I had been shown. 'Many end up fitting out G.R.P. hulls,' I was told. 'In the old days ten men might work on a boat; nowadays, it takes probably three to complete a boat.'

The two brothers, carrying on their father's dream to own a boat yard because he loved boats, also show his flair for innovation. They told me that, due to their concern for the environment, they had designed and built a fleet of new electric boats. These Phœnix 21s are replacing the older electric boats. I have seen these on the Northern rivers many times in the last two seasons. They have caused no problems to me in my tiny sailing dinghy *Wanderbug,* as we pass by; and their greatly reduced noise level, less wash and lower speeds, are greatly appreciated, and must be a great asset both to the fauna and flora of the area, as well as to other boat-users.

The return of Broadland to an era where boats are owned and restored by local boat-builders, with new wooden-boat order books

A Phoenix electric cruiser, a boat for the future

at an encouraging level, is a welcome sign for the water-based industries in Broadland. Hopefully, it will restore to the Broads its outstanding beauty and dignity for sailing, that once we were in danger of losing.

Even as this book was going to press I found out more to interest me in the Richardson family. Last weekend was the 'Three Rivers Race'. So bad was the weather that over one hundred boats did not finish. Out of the fleet that endured a violent storm, then a long, windless, cold, wet night, which made the race a real test of endurance, the Slipstream class, designed by Mick years ago, gained second and fourth places.

Mardling in the Greyhound Pub the following day, I heard a man congratulate Mick. 'Your son did very well,' he said. 'He only came fourth,' replied Mick, a proud father. 'Why did the *Slipstream* do so well?' I asked. 'It's a very pretty boat, and it's designed by a clever man,' said the man. He had sailed *Beth* and was well qualified to appreciate her sailing qualities.

My husband bought our Wayfarer before trying one because, as an engineer, he could appreciate that 'if it looks right, it is right'. Mick, also an engineer, commented 'My tutor at Loughborough College said, 'If it *looks* right, it can be mathematically proved that it *is* right.' The *Slipstream* proved the point.

John Perryman

John was born in Shoreham in 1934. His father took him afloat for his first sea passage in the family motor cruiser at the age of three months. His grandfather was a master mariner who sailed a square-rigger out of Liverpool. The family moved to Derby in 1935 and John and his father spent much time afloat in *Typhoon*, a thirty-foot-long, ketch-rigged, converted lifeboat. John remembers being able to scull and steer long before he learnt to ride a bicycle.

Starting work at fifteen years, with the idea of going into a drawing office, John soon realized that his main interest was in boats. In 1950, the family sold up and made *Typhoon* their home. Setting off from Trent Locks along the river to Lincoln, then Boston, and finally, to Yarmouth, John's father found work in Yarmouth town. His son was taken on at Herbert Woods' boat yard. He proudly remembers that he was 'Jimmy Turner's boy', and that his first task was winding caulking cotton. 'I was in heaven,' he said. He also remembers that he was the only apprentice who travelled to work by boat. The family were living aboard *Typhoon* in Woods' yard at the time. John's enthusiasm was so great that Mr Cliff Patchett persuaded Mr Woods to take the boy on as an indentured apprentice, which meant that he got one shilling a week tool money. Jimmy Turner's crew consisted of Sam Cooke (Snoo), Gordon Allen (Maggot), Sid Bensley (Spider) and John (Pudden). Jimmy suggested that John should rig his dinghy and go sailing at the newly-formed Hickling Sailing Club. John Loynes, the yard designer, prepared a sail plan and Herbert Woods gave John space, in the old shed No.1, to fit *Spray* out for serious sailing. His crew at that time was Pat Beales, Waldo's daughter. 'That was a wonderful time for a young couple,' reflected John, 'no drugs or vices, just sailing, boating and adventuring'. *Spray* won three cups in her first season, and the young couple visited many of the local regattas in *Typhoon*.

Not long after starting at Woods', Mr Patchett suggested to John that he might be interested in joining a City and Guilds course on yachting and boat-building. He and Leslie Landamore were promoting the idea that every apprentice on the Broads should sign up. John completed the course, gaining highest mark in the area.

In his own words, John described life at the boat yard in the '50s.

I worked with Jimmy's crew on the building of several Norfolk dinghies, Twilight class yachts, St George class hire cruisers, Gay Lady class yachts and three sea-going craft designed by Arthur Robb, a most eminent yacht designer of the time.

The yawl *Rob Roy*, designed by Arthur Robb, built by H. Woods Ltd. - Jimmy Turner standing in the cockpit, John Perryman sitting.

The work force was drawn from the surrounding villages and the yard was a village in itself. Surplus food stuffs to be sold or traded were a regular feature. Rabbit and pheasant in season came from the Hickling contingent and a fry-up of herring or sweet beach-caught codling would come in from a chap who lived at Winterton. Jack Findlay, an engineer, was also a bookie's runner for the yard and another, whose name escapes me, did a bit of haircutting in the rigger's shop in the lunch hour. Freddie King was the rigger. He could splice wire like it was spaghetti. He was the on-shore lifeboat mechanic at Caister and had one eye. He lost the other when Mr Hitler dropped a bomb on his trawler and blew him and his wheel-house over the side.

The management decided, one day, that we should get modern and have a tractor for hauling boats about the yard. A 'Field Marshal' diesel machine arrived and Alf Cook (Cookie), the haul-out foreman, appointed himself as driver. The tractor was started by inserting a cartridge into a fitting on the cylinder head, striking it with the hammer provided and the resulting explosion would fire the cylinder. Cookie did this but failed to secure the cartridge. It fired and shot out, smashed through the rigger's shop door, gave Freddie a hell of a shock and shot out through the far wall!

The first time we had a go at making a 'fibreglass' dinghy we got it all wrong and the resins self-combusted and set fire to the paint shop!

Most winters I spent some time repairing boats in company with Herbert Walter Woods. The sheds were gloomy, lighting being by individual lead lights held by each worker. The water was invariably ankle deep and sometimes covered in ice. I have memories of all four of us working away under those conditions when Walter would start up a hymn with the rest of us joining in. 'There is a green hill far away' was a favourite. It was an eerie, almost surrealist scene with these unprepossessing salts o' the earth working away in the gloom singing hymns. It must have been like that 1,000 years ago when the ancestors of these men were building churches.

Lou Green was an ex-wherryman and sometimes when he was just thinking about a job he would hum a tune to himself and do a wherryman's step dance. (I have never seen it done since.) This consisted of tiny restricted step movements such as could be done in the well of a wherry.

Walter was a master helmsman and raced the Woods family Yarmouth O.D. *White Damsel* with devastating success. For this he wore his yachting rig - pin-stripe suit and a cloth cap. Apart from being a canny helmsman he was fearless. *Damsel* with her 'pot hunter' rig was a handful in a breeze and Walter with a grim face would charge through the fleet at Potter regatta with a cry of 'look out tergether, I'm a coming trow,' and if anyone complained he would grumble 'yer shouldn't have been there'. I crewed him often enough to know the routine.

This idyllic way of life was interrupted when John was called up for National Service. He left suffering from chronic hay fever and, returning home, designed and built two sixteen-foot angling boats for Waldo Beales, *Trucie* and *Coypu*. Joining forces with Mick

72

Richardson, he built *Brer Rabbit,* with the intention of starting a hire fleet, and John recalls during this time mixing with and

enjoying the company of Norfolk boating people, all making their living from the water. Being with Billy May, Tommy Moore, Derek Gibbs,Derwood Wright, and Sid Wren, to name just a few, was most enjoyable. However, meeting Ian Nicolson, at the bar of the Broads Haven changed John's

Trucie and *Coypu*

life. As a result of that meeting, John's ambition to move into yacht design was realized when he joined the design office of Alan Buchanan. Time spent designing wood and steel-deep water-racing yachts, and having the opportunity to crew on them, was most satisfying.

He met and married Constance, who was nanny to the Buchanan children, and the couple moved to the south coast, where John worked as a marine surveyor. The next move was to work at Brooke Marine, and new areas of knowledge, such as estimating, tendering, contract management, shipyard procedures, government contracts and slush funds were mastered.

Then came the opportunity to set up in business alone. An office was set up in Lowestoft, and with a fellow draughtsman from Brooke Marine, the two men set up a plan to get orders for designing commercial craft by travelling abroad, mainly to the eastern Mediterranean and offering tenders jointly with Broads yards. Possibly the most glamorous job was building the seventy-five-foot express luxury motor yacht *Najwan,* for one of the Kuwaiti princes, and the largest design was a one-hundred-foot royal yacht for the Emir of Doha. These and other luxury power craft were arranged in conjunction with Powles International of Wroxham.

John recalled the excitement of the chase for contracts abroad. 'There was little to match the feeling of bribing some Arab telex operator in the dead of night, in some cockroach-ridden hotel, to

Najwan II, luxury motor yacht built for royalty in Kuwait

send our coded message back to Alan in the office "Nuts for Xmas",
meaning that we had finalized a contract for some royal yacht or
patrol boat...also the rush of adrenalin when sketching out the
details for the seventy-five-foot royal yacht on the insides of several
fag packets, whilst camping with the Beduin in the desert.'

    This exciting and stressful lifestyle came to an end eventually.
John's partner went to Canada, John closed his office and went to
work at George Prior Engineering as an estimator and contract
manager. Whilst he was there, they planned to meet the need for a
ship capable of dismasting, dismantling and removing redundant oil
rigs, but before the design could be built, oil hit rock bottom prices
and over one hundred men were stood off at Prior's. John returned
to the drawing board, and did a couple of joint ventures with
Prior's, supplying small commercial craft to Crown agents contracts.
In John's words:

The last of these was to be, perhaps, my most mentally rewarding of all the
boats that I have designed. It was a 58-foot all-aluminium open surf boat
for the Pitcairn Island community. Pitcairn is not an idyllic atoll with
sandy beaches. It is a lump of rock sticking straight out of the Pacific -

Pitcairn Island surf boat designed by John Perryman

sheer cliffs and no beach. The only landing is a tiny cove about 50 feet wide straight on to a patch of stones. The Pacific rollers - 20 feet high - pound this tiny inlet most of the time. Since Fletcher Christian landed on the island they have used a long succession of frail wooden boats for the job of fishing and, in later years, collecting stores from passing shops.

The requirement was for a metal boat capable of working in these terrific seas. I chose the hull form of a Norfolk beach lifeboat rigged with a wherry-type sail on the main mast, a Bermudan mizzen and a very powerful engine.

It worked so well that the islanders made voyages to nearby Henderson Island to haul logs to make carvings for the tourist trade, and voyaged 3,000 miles to New Zealand and Tahiti. My boat gave the islanders a new freedom and, most important of all, an escape boat in the event of an island disaster. So good was the boat that they ordered another exactly the same!

John retired in the late 1990s, feeling that the European Recreational Craft Directive would cause chaos in the boating industry. However he still retains an active interest in the Maritime Museum in Yarmouth; he was a founder member, helping to establish it on the sea front. Also he still takes an interest in *Albion,* one that goes back some thirty-five years. He was chairman of the Wherry Trust for eight years. He and Constance still sail *Spray*. *Wanderbug* and *Spray* passed one another on a glorious sailing day last year, so I met *Spray* before I met Mr and Mrs Perryman, which is the way I like it to be.

In reflective mood, as we mardled at the excellent Greyhound pub at Hickling, John reminisced, 'When working in wood, if you didn't get it right in the first boat, you could adapt the lines or alter the rake, to achieve more speed or a better balance in the next boat. Now, with G.R.P. production, there is much greater investment at stake, and you have to accept that once a boat is designed, the moulds are the radical design, and hundreds of boats will be turned out exactly the same.'

John Perryman with a model of the *Albion*